HEROES OF F

BY

STUART R BROGAN

Published by:

Midgard Books
Glastonbury
England
www.midgardbooks.co.uk

Visit our online retailer for all things Viking, Heathen & Pagan

www.shield-maiden.co.uk

Copyright © 2015 Stuart R Brogan

All Artwork Copyright © 2015 Stuart R Brogan

1st Printed Edition December 2015

All rights reserved. No part of this publication may be reproduced, stored in a retrieval system, or transmitted in any form or by any means without the prior permission of the publisher, nor be otherwise circulated in any form of binding or cover other than that which it has been published and without a similar condition being imposed on the subsequent purchaser.

ACKNOWLEDGEMENTS

First and foremost I would like to thank you, the reader, for purchasing this book. Without you I wouldn't be doing what I am doing.

Many thanks to my Mother, Father and Brother for their continuous faith and support, and to my fellow Heathen Warriors – Rich, Pete, Jon, Steve, Dean and Liam.

Thanks also to:

Autumn at The Wordsmith Desk for the excellent editing and formatting skills; Sifu Clive Whitworth and Paul from ITG Northampton for the top quality instruction in the RAT system; Jeet Kune Do and Kali; Ben at Courtyard Books; Kate at Pagan Dawn Magazine; Northern Runes Radio in Canada; Jack Salyer in Germany for his kind and humbling words, all those who have given support and encouragement and The Tunnel for giving me stress relief.

I raise a toast to the ancestors who paved the way through turbulent times and still held strong to their beliefs and way of life. To the High Ones, whom I stand before on my own two feet as a free man:

Hail to you!

DEDICATION

To my wife Fiona, the greatest shield maiden a man could have, this is for you.

I love you.

TABLE OF CONTENTS

Introduction 1

Acclaim for *Heathen Warrior* 8

Arwald 10

Beowulf 16

Boudicca 24

Corineus 33

Cú Chulainn 40

Hengest and Horsa 47

Hereward the Wake 53

Herne the Hunter 63

Jack the Giant Killer 69

King Arthur 76

Merlin 87

Morgan le Fay 93

Robin Hood 101

Scáthach 112

Wayland the Smith 119

Widukind 126

The Final Chapter 132

HEROES OF PAGAN BRITAIN

BY

STUART R BROGAN

INTRODUCTION

Wassail ladies and gentlemen, I humbly invite you to come and bear witness to a veritable feast of terrorists, criminals, outlaws and rebels. Stand amazed; behold in wonder and gaze upon a gaggle of individuals, who, throughout the history of this magical land have upset the status quo, defied Kings, stood their ground in the face of injustice and danced to their own tune. A motley crew, who refused to bend to the will of those who believed themselves to be superior, individuals stood against those who wished to force tyrannical laws upon the already downtrodden populace. Let's be honest here: the powers that be—regardless of the era of which we speak—would have us revel in such negative descriptions regarding those of defiant spirit, confident in the notion that the "brainwashed" masses will demonize and rebuke such behaviour. In turn, they'd steer our attention from the causes and reasoning that made these people act in such a way, a clever trick to distract the majority from the ills that truly plague us still utilised by today's governments. But there are those throughout history who have seen the bigger picture, those who have sifted the information and have truly seen what was happening around us, and delving deeper among them are the one percent, the brave few that are willing to stand up and fight back! They are the defenders, the true of heart, and the heroes!

The heroic idea of standing your ground against crippling odds fills some of us with dread and others with joy. Some thrive on the fight. It defines them; it gives them a cause, thus giving their lives meaning and separating them from the "norm"; but how would any of us acted if we had lived in such turbulent historical times? Would we have had the courage not just to say, "NO!" or "We will not take this anymore!" but to put everything we hold dear on the line and take up arms? I would like to give a concrete, categorical "Yes!", but of course I don't truly know how I would have reacted faced with such adversity. Some Earth-based religious folk amongst you may say our modern day equivalent of a Pagan hero may very well be the Eco Activist doing battle with unscrupulous corporations that are ruining our planet and ecosystem. In my mind's eye there is a difference between an environmental activist in today's world and a beleaguered serf rising up against his/her oppressors in the Dark Ages. Of course that's not to say that I belittle any activist standing up for his/her beliefs nowadays; in fact I respect and salute them for having the courage of their convictions and taking the fight to the oppressor. So we ask ourselves, who are these godlike warriors of virtue—are they what history depicts or are they normal people placed in extraordinary situations, forced to act outside of their normal comfort zone? Are the stories we have been spoon-fed by scholars and historians factually based or are they nothing more than folklore told as a tonic to ease the social fears of that time? In our valiant quest to find out we shall explore and dissect the information available. I shall become Sherlock Holmes and you my trusted Watson, once more embarking on a glorious and hazardous adventure, to weed out the truth from the smoke and mirrors we know as history! Of course that's not to say that we shall find the answers we seek; we may just be left scratching our heads with more questions.

So back to the task in hand. The aim of the book is to explore the rich tapestry of characters that have made an impact within the Pagan religion based in the British Isles. Some are claimed to be fictional, others based in fact and some we just haven't got a clue either way—this by its very definition could prove controversial. Along the way there will be opposing views and theories from all different walks of life. There will be hypothesis given that may seem outlandish and possibly even crazy, but as an open minded kind of chap I feel all avenues should be explored before being dismissed because let's face it: how many crazy Pagans do you know who state they consort with Fairy folk on a regular basis or claim to have a house Elf living under the stairs? (If you do have an Elf hostage please don't forget to feed him/her.)I must state that this of course does not mean that I agree with all the ideas put forward but I will, however, chime in with my own theory at the end of each chapter. You may agree or disagree with the conclusion at which I arrive but to put it bluntly, this is of no consequence to me. So I state clearly one more time: I am not trying to say that my conclusion is right but to explore all ideas then use my thoughts as a mere footnote to the chapter. Basically, don't bother writing to proclaim, "This man is a crackpot; what a stupid theory!" because that is not what the book is about.

I have also endeavoured to research more unknown or less known folk from our Pagan past. There are those that most of us will be familiar with but in the course of choosing my heroes I stumbled upon some that I had not heard of or those of whom I had limited knowledge. I have to admit, even though I class myself as a Heathen I was shocked and embarrassed about how little I truly knew regarding Paganism in the U.K. I was, however, pleasantly surprised with some of the characters I investigated and completely in awe of others; some of their tales even brought a tear to my eye. It was a challenging experience preparing for this book for it required far more extensive research than my previous work *Heathen Warrior*. My first foray into the wild world of literary creation was a personal book told from a pragmatic and experienced viewpoint using my own stories as a basis of investigation. The book you are now reading is by far more objective in its reasoning and is multi-faceted due to a multitude of ideas and opinions acquired from a host of different sources.

I hope this book encourages you to do some investigating of your own, to go to your local museum and scour the records for ancient clues revealing age-old secrets regarding our Pagan past or even to embark on a literary adventure of your own, possibly writing your own book. As with all my books I will state that I am no expert and would never claim to be. In my humble opinion it is impossible to be an expert when dealing with history or spirituality because regarding the former, we were not there and the latter, it is not tangible. We can only make educated guesses based on the limited information we have and even then it will be biased based on our own morality and motivations. I always akin it to this: at a murder trial you have the defence and the prosecution; both have "expert" witnesses to add weight and academic prowess to their case. The same "evidence" is examined by both parties yet each will reach a different conclusion to support their individual perspective. Surely if they are both "experts" looking at the same evidence they would reach the same conclusion? The evidence hasn't changed. Food for thought, I feel.

With such a verity and rich history from which to choose, I started with a rather large list but soon realised that I should be picky regarding those I included. It would become apparent that an entire book could be written on most, if not all of the characters. What follows is my "Hotlist" of those I found to be of worthy of inclusion.

With this in mind I think it is about time we cracked on with our newest adventure, to explore Pagan Britain and those who have gone down in history as its advocates. They say that one man's terrorist is another man's freedom fighter depending on what side of the fence you are sitting. By the end of each chapter you will have to make your choice and figure out on which side you are sitting. I know I have. To conclude this introduction I shall leave you with a fantastic, morally justifiable and I believe, apt quote from Ridley Scott's movie *Robin Hood*. So sit back, relax and prepare for one hell of a ride!

"In times of tyranny and injustice when law oppresses the people, the outlaw takes his place in history."

ACCLAIM FOR *HEATHEN WARRIOR*

"Heathen Warrior may indeed help re-enliven an interest in the ancient warrior traditions of Europe."

4/5 Wyldwood Radio, England

"Might be seen in ways as a present-day incarnation of The Hávamál."

***Brigid's Fire Magazine**, Ireland*

"Highly recommended."

Dr Liz Williams, PhD in Philosophy of Science & International SciFi Author

4.5 / 5 Stars

Amazon.com

"Brogan has done a terrific job in producing a guide that manages to be deeply thought-provoking and spiritual, yet at the same time utterly rooted in the real world. I

very much hope we'll be hearing more from him in the future."

Kate Large, Editor, *Pagan Dawn Magazine*

CHAPTER ONE

ARWALD

Our first hero is Arwald, known by historians as the last Pagan king of Anglo Saxon England before the Vikings turned up in the 9th century. In truth, most of what we know of this man is from Bede's classic, historical epic *Historia ecclesiastica gentis Anglorum*. Whilst he did chronicle a lot of information regarding the Anglo Saxons we must remember he was a Christian, thus his view may be slightly one-sided. Apparently Arwald was a devout Pagan from Jutish decent and went to war with the Wessex Saxon King Caedwalla when he invaded the Isle of Wight to not only try and Christianize it but to engage in ethnic cleansing, his intent to purge the Island of Pagans and replace the populace with those loyal to him and the church. It is also said that Caedwalla had promised half the island to St Wilfrid and the church no doubt in a bid to guarantee his place in the afterlife. Despite the military might levelled against him, Arwald refused to back down in the face of Christian aggression and was fully prepared to fight for his Pagan faith and folk. As I was born in Southampton, a city on the south coast of England and situated across the Solent from the Isle of Wight, I feel a little miffed and embarrassed that I had never heard of this Arwald fellow because not only was he a local King but a man who seems to have personified the qualities of a Pagan hero. When I was at school I remember visiting many museums in the area to investigate and learn all about the Anglo Saxons who had colonised the area in the years 400 – 1066. At this point in history it was not called Southampton but known as *Hamwic* and according to historical records was regarded as a market town and located across the River Itchen in what is now known as St Marys. I mention this because records show that it was a planned homestead and was obviously held in high regard; in turn it would become very wealthy and very powerful in the Anglo Saxon world. When we examine Caedwalla's motives for invasion we see that it was very probably multi-reasoned. Firstly, it was and still is a very busy port, bringing goods from all around the world and also acted as the Royal mint for several Saxon kings until it was relocated to Winchester in the late 9th century. Thus trade was imperative with other tribes, kings and countries and most would only trade with those of the same faith, i.e., Christianity. Secondly, in a tribal society such as the Anglo Saxons, a king could be seen as being weak with such a Pagan presence going "unchecked" on his doorstep. I'm sure the Church would have given Caedwalla a gentle nudge regarding the "Lord's" wishes appertaining to the Pagan neighbours. Thirdly, I believe that it would have been strategic in the sense of the geographical location of the island itself. Not only was it extra land to grow crops and raise cattle, etc., but also a valuable military lookout post across the Solent towards mainland Europe. If anyone reading this has ever visited the island you will know that its vantage point is outstanding across the channel.

When and where the war took place is still open for debate. However, what we do know is that the death toll was extremely high; I would wager on both sides. Arwald himself died during the battle. It is said that Arwald's two younger brothers managed to escape the battle and seek refuge in the Great Ytene Forest–Ytenes meaning *"Jutish"*. It is now known as the New Forest just across the Solent to the west. In my opinion, this is highly probable due to the close proximity of the forest to the island. The brothers stood a good chance of survival in the forest because at this period in history it covered a large area and would probably have held some sympathisers to the Pagan cause. However, Bede states that the brothers were betrayed to King Caedwalla who was in hiding in an area now known as Stoneham, just a few miles north of Southampton city centre, dying of the wounds he had received at the hands of Pagan resistance. Bede goes on to tell us that just before the brothers were due to be put to the sword, an abbot stepped in and they both converted to Christianity. In an ironic twist in the tale, the brothers' names were not recorded; however, after they converted they later became known collectively at St Arwald! At this point I have to point out some contradictions in the tale. In some accounts they were not Arwald's brothers at all but nephews, so we don't really know for sure who exactly they were or if they even existed or whether it was nothing more than a bit of Christian PR work to appease the masses.

Regarding Arwald's dynasty back on the Isle of Wight, it is said that the only survivor of the Jutes was Arwald's sister, whose name is unknown and was not recorded by Bede. What we do know is at this time she was married to Egbert, King of Kent, who was another Jute King at war with Caedwalla and his brother, Mul. It is recorded that she was an ancestor of King Alfred the Great who would go on to defend England against the Heathen Vikings! It would appear that Arwald's fight was, at first glance, utterly pointless, nothing more than delaying the inevitable. He had lost his kingdom and life; his brothers converted to Christianity and his sister was married to a Christian king who became a blood relation to arguably Britain's first "famous" Christian King, and not forgetting the Isle of Wight falling to the whims of the "new" religion. So was it worth it? Well in my opinion, yes it was. Arwald shows us that even though we may face unfathomable odds and in our heart of hearts know that we fight ideology as well as physical battles, we must stand tall with honour and resolve. We realise we might never win or if we do it would not be without a huge personal sacrifice, but when faced with this knowledge we stand our ground regardless. That, in my opinion, is the essence of a hero.

Sticking with the Anglo Saxon theme, this brings us to our next hero, the most famous one of all, a name synonymous with the warrior and heroic ideals in this period of history: Beowulf.

CHAPTER TWO
BEOWULF

I would wager any amount of money that everyone reading this book has heard the name Beowulf at some point in their lives; in fact, I would happily bet the meagre contents of my wallet that you couldn't find many who haven't heard the name even outside of the Pagan community. Granted, most outside of the Pagan community would know that there have been Hollywood movies based on the Anglo Saxon superhero. However, beyond the name, how many could state where and when the hero appears or that he is, in fact, the main star in what is universally agreed to be the pinnacle of Anglo Saxon literature, a manuscript known as the *Nowell Codex*? The poem itself is only a part of the Codex; scholars and historians estimate the epic poem was written somewhere between the 8th and 11th centuries. Its author, however, has eluded even the most ardent historic investigator. Also, until the end of the 18th century it was largely ignored and unstudied and only really came to prominence when it was published in 1815 in an edition prepared by the Icelandic-Danish scholar Grímur Jónsson Thorkelin. I find it odd that such a valuable manuscript was left undiscovered and overlooked for such a long period of time but it has certainly made up for it since, firing the imaginations of the young and old alike. In fact, here in the U.K there is a resurgence of interest in the Anglo Saxon world, possibly due to the discovery of many a Saxon treasure around the British Isles or the enduring allure of that famous Saxon burial mound: Sutton Hoo.

It would appear that the poem itself is set in the 5th century and focuses on our hero's battles, both during his up-and-coming younger years and then as he becomes older, right up to his death. The main premise and backbone of the story seems to be Beowulf travelling far and wide to prove his superior strength and guile by fighting and defeating monsters and generally showing everyone how super "macho" he is! Joking aside, having read *Beowulf* I personally see social and ethical themes woven into the story line: fidelity, loyalty and friendship, as well as the typical heroic elements so prominent in the Saxon period. Of course such hero elements were vital to the aural storytelling in this moment in history as the hero was not only the pinnacle of manhood but was also a major part within the spiritual and religious context. Whether or not this was intended by the author we shall never know; maybe I am just stating the obvious or maybe it's just storytelling in its most basic form. Whatever the reason, the poem itself gives us a hero that all men want to be and all women want to be with! It gives us stunning settings in Northern Europe, epic battles and thrilling adventures that fire our imaginations and make us daydream of glorious victories, or on the flipside, makes us think, "Thank goodness I'm not fighting big, scary monsters and I am nice and safe, tucked up on my sofa!"

The narration of the poem begins with our hero, Beowulf, a famous warrior from the Geats in Scandinavia who comes to the help of Hroðgar, the King of the Danes, whose mead hall located in Heorot has been under attack by a man-eating monster known as Grendel. (It is implied that the attacks have been going on for some time.) The king is at a loss as to how the beast can be defeated and has lost a vast amount of warriors at the hands of evil blight, thus forcing the king to summon the mightiest of warriors: Beowulf. The action begins with Beowulf and his men pretending to be asleep within the mead hall, anxiously awaiting the monster to attack. It is even noted that Beowulf refuses to be armed, stating it would be an unfair advantage over the beast! In this one, sweeping, heroic statement we as the reader can marvel at the sheer confidence and—dare I say—borderline arrogance, displayed by our hero. And that's the point isn't it, to make us put aside our own fears and follow this brave warrior into the fray? After a ferocious battle, Beowulf slays the fiend, killing him using his bare hands but then, straight from the script of a Hollywood movie and in a fit of rage at losing her "son" Grendel's mother swears revenge and attacks the hall, furiously kills a few warriors then retreats to her lair located under a nearby lake. Not to be outdone, our hero tracks and engages in mortal combat with her and after a torturous battle she is despatched at the hands of our Dark Age superhero by utilising a giant sword that he himself finds in the mother's lair—or more to the point—he chops off her head.

Victorious, and obviously enjoying the fame and rewards that being a "super warrior" can bring,

Beowulf returns triumphantly home to Geatland in Sweden and later becomes King of the Geats. After a period of fifty years has passed (and from what we can gather not a lot happening), Beowulf's kingdom comes under sustained attack from a dragon that was awoken by a slave stealing his gold. In heroic style, Beowulf sets forth with a small band of warriors to engage and kill the dragon, but is unsuccessful. It would appear that most of his men either are killed or retreat while only two dare to remain with him: Wiglaf, a relation, and a warrior known as Tinshaw. Beowulf decides to enter the dragon's lair and fight him where he would least expect it. Of course in true heroic style Beowulf defeats the dragon, but is fatally wounded in the ensuing battle. After his death, his attendants bury him in a tumulus (burial mound) on vast cliffs overlooking the sea in Geatland. Of course this would have symbolic meaning in terms of Beowulf "looking out" and "protecting" the kingdom from invaders, as well as a focal point for weary travellers casting their gaze up as they approach by sea, overlooked by the mightiest of heroes. As a passing note, my boyhood daydream was to be the one who found the long lost tomb of Beowulf and all the treasures held within, to hold aloft his magical sword and to connect with the very essence of Anglo Saxon folklore. But alas, it was not to be. Will we ever find tangible proof of his existence? Should we actively hunt for it? Or should we just bathe in the fantasy handed down for generations? As with many things in life, perception is an individual thing.

When we take a step back one cannot help but notice the glaringly obvious similarities between *Beowulf* and JRR Tolkien's *The Hobbit* or *Lord of the Rings*—warriors, dragons, epic battles, mythical creatures, folk lore and magic. Of course it is common knowledge that Tolkien based a lot of his characters and storylines on ancient Anglo Saxon and old Norse lore and was indeed himself an avid fan of all things "Dark Age". But no matter how much we can see on the surface, there is so much more woven through all of Tolkien's work. There are many social truths and dilemmas that we face today and problems regarding our interaction with others around us. There are spiritual crises that make us question our "Gods" and "Goddesses" and of course nods to the great Pagan heroes that have captivated scholars and historians for years.

In my opinion, the epic known as *Beowulf* is what started the "Fighting Fantasy" genre. It alone is the most utilised reference point when creating sweeping majestic heroes, complete with human flaws. I personally cannot think of any fantasy book or movie that can't somehow be compared to, or wasn't inspired by *Beowulf*. Off the top of my head I can recall the famous mead hall scene from one of my favourite movies, *The 13th Warrior*: the mead hall, pretending to be asleep, half-man half-beasts and following them into their lair, sound familiar? When we take a deeper look at the narrative we see that it is similar to the script of a modern movie, the three big fights being the three main acts in the film. It is as if it were written for the silver screen. Coincidences and frivolity aside, we can see for ourselves why this in itself is a testament to the enduring legacy of Anglo Saxon literature and the relevance it has in the here-and-now, not only the Pagan world but in society as a whole. Modern life has us yearning for more, not more in the sense of materialistic objectivity, but more in the sense of spiritual and ethical fulfilment. It is true that Beowulf had an ego and that he craved fortune and fame along with wealth but that's what resonates with us, the fact that he was only human and yet still achieved great things. I have mentioned this hypothesis before in my previous book *Heathen Warrior* and still believe it holds sway. It is my belief that *Beowulf* holds such importance within today's technology-obsessed world that it will be reimagined, retold, made into movies and TV shows long after I am dust and to be honest, I think that is fantastic. If only the unknown author had realised what a legacy he was leaving and what an influence his words would have.

It's not just the men that can lead others into glorious battle; there have been women in history that have made such a mark as to reverberate through history itself. Our first woman needs no other introduction other than her name: Boudicca.

CHAPTER THREE
BOUDICCA

We have all heard the saying, "behind every great man is a greater woman" and our next subject is, in the eyes of some, a very great woman indeed. In fact this woman very nearly brought the Roman Empire to its knees on the British Isles. Ruthlessly adept in warfare and tactics she is for many the poster girl for equal rights within the "warrior" culture and, I have to say, a personal favourite of mine. She was a woman forced into action when all was taken from her, a woman who refused to bow down before her oppressors and vowed to bring justice to her people and make those responsible pay for their indiscretions. Her name was Boudicca: queen of the Iceni tribe, one of Britain's most venerated heroes and a woman who more than qualifies to be on our list.

The year is AD 43 and Britain was not yet the collective "United" Kingdom we all know. There was no one single ruler or king and the country was divided into separate kingdoms, each occupied by a dominate tribe and led by its own independent ruler. His /her subjects followed this regional "king/queen" with unwavering loyalty and it has been described that in some instances the leader was deemed to be able to claim direct lineage from the Gods and Goddesses themselves. In the eastern part of the country, in what is now East Anglia, lived the Iceni tribe. The Iceni were widely known to be fiercely independent and from what we can tell very well respected and feared in equal measure. At this period in history we must also understand that even though there were mild skirmishes between tribes there was no, what we would call, "wars" by today's standards. There was neither real solidarity between tribes or clans and alliances were short-lived; that was about to change in the wake of Roman arrogance.

Boudicca was a tribal queen and was married to Prasutagus, the then-ruler of the Iceni people. When the Romans conquered the tribes in southern England in AD 43, they begrudgingly allowed Prasutagus to continue to rule. However, when Prasutagus died the Romans decided to rule the Iceni directly and confiscated the property of the leading tribesmen. Up until this point there had been an uneasy truce and peace between the tribes, as all despised the Romans. As to hammer home the point of Roman dominance it is widely believed that they are said to have stripped and flogged Boudicca then raped her daughters in front of the tribe and refused to acknowledge Boudicca's status. We must bear in mind that due to the tribes' loyalty and perception of their leaders at this time, this would have been an unbearable shame and an affront to the Gods and Goddesses themselves. The very fabric of these "unholy" and "sacrilegious" acts would have rocked the very foundations of tribal society and for all intents and purposes the world was crashing down around them. Most normal people would bow and crack under such treatment; however, these actions not only exacerbated widespread resentment at Roman rule but started to stoke the fires of rebellion in the bellies of not only the Iceni but all of the southern tribes. All they needed was a leader.

History books tell us that Boudicca stepped up to the plate and started to unify the tribes under the banner of freedom instigated by her treatment and spurred on by her fierce anti-Roman rhetoric. Many historians believe there were a few minor battles but it wasn't really until 60 or 61 AD, while the Roman governor Gaius Suetonius Paullinus was leading a campaign in North Wales to take care of the "Druid" problem, that the Iceni utilised the opportunity and rebelled enmasse. It wasn't just the Iceni though; many members of other tribes including the Trinovantes decided to flock to her banner and joined them for her declaration of war against the hated Romans. I believe that the Romans were arrogant and couldn't comprehend the idea that the tribes would join forces, let alone revolt and fight back, thus they didn't leave adequate forces in the area to keep order if such an unthinkable thing should happen. However, the Romans were about to get taught a lesson, a lesson that tells us that you can only whip a dog a certain amount of times before the dog bites back. And bite back it did—hard.

Boudicca's warriors successfully marched on and defeated the then-infamous Roman Ninth Legion, then laid waste to the then-capital of Roman Britain, Colchester. Colchester at this time was the location for the temple dedicated to the emperor Claudius and as such was an extremely important place, holding a vast amount of relevance within

Roman high society. It is also worth pointing out that the settlement was the place where discharged Roman soldiers would go. In my mind this means that Boudicca was not up against fresh-faced recruits but battle-seasoned troops who one would expect to have some seriously impressive skills regarding warfare. Yet she didn't even bat an eye at such odds; was she insane? It would appear that this wasn't such an issue because the Celtic army laid waste to Colchester and some reports suggest they pretty much killed everyone! After destroying the Roman Empires flagship city, Boudicca's army then went on to destroy London, even though some had fled from Colchester, including the Roman commander Gaius Suetonius Paulinus. Knowing London was her next intended target, the warning did little good. It is said most people evacuated on hearing the news that she was on her way, thus leaving it easy pickings for the ferocious Celt. Again, Boudicca's army decimated London and raised it to the ground. It is said that even to this day if you dig down deep enough you can find evidence of ash dating back to the time of Boudicca!

However, the party was not to last. The Romans regrouped somewhere in the West Midlands, led by Gaius Suetonius Paulinus and despite being heavily outnumbered, eventually defeated Boudicca at what historians call the Battle of Watling Street, located (some suggest) at Wroxeter, Shropshire. However, it remains speculative due to the fact that we are relying on Roman sources. We all know that history is written by the victor and in all probability it's been warped by their own views regarding the revolt. It is also recorded that the Roman commander chose his battle ground well and any experienced soldier would know to use the surrounding countryside to his advantage.

Apparently (according to Tacitus, a Roman scholar) the battle was fought in a narrow gorge with a dense forest to the rear that would stop any flanking manoeuvre employed by the Celts. The gorge would funnel the Celts in, and with their numbers, make attack easier to defend against, a tactic successfully employed for centuries including by the Spartans at Thermopylae in 480 BC. We must also presume that not only were the Roman Legions better trained but also they were better equipped with regards to weaponry and armour.

We do know that the Celts did not favour armour and only had spears, shields and scramsax (small knives) and more than anything were relying on sheer numbers, adrenaline-fuelled bravery and most of all, their fearless leader to guide them to victory.

There have been many ideas put forward regarding the actual location of the battle. In March 2010 evidence was published suggesting the site may be located at Church Stowe, Northamptonshire. The Kennet Valley, close to Silchester, has also been thrown into the ring as a candidate for the site of the battle, but in truth we really don't know.

It is worth mentioning that even though Boudicca was defeated, her victories sent shock waves through the Roman Empire. In fact the Emperor Nero actually contemplated withdrawing his forces from the British Isles for fear of another uprising. It had shown the Britons and the rest of the world that Rome could be defeated and were not indestructible as the Roman press machine would have you believe. The defeat of Boudicca ensured Roman rule in the southern half of Britain; however, up in the wilds of northern Britain the situation remained volatile. In AD 69, a noble by the name of Venutius from the Brigantes tribe would lead another less well-documented revolt. Apparently, it had started initially as a tribal rivalry but soon evolved, becoming anti-Roman in nature, but again with little or next to no evidence we are left clutching at straws and formulating hypothesis based on conjecture and folklore.

So what happened to this warrior queen? Well, historians tell us that after she lost the war she poisoned herself rather than have been taken as a trophy of war, and no doubt have been paraded around Rome and Europe as a visual reminder of Roman dominance. I can see her point; she had lost everything and there was never going to be a favourable outcome if she had fallen into the clutches of her enemies, so she was left with only one option, to end it on her terms. I personally think it was extremely courageous for her to take that course of action but I believe that before embarking on such a destructive path she would have made peace with her destiny and possibly had even realised that this course of action was possible when she first started the rebellion.

Boudicca's legacy lives on to this day. From Victorian queens being her namesake to huge statues built in her honour, she is so interwoven within the social identity of Britain that she has become a household name. In poetry, literature, film and even placed on coinage this formidable warrior truly is a hero of Pagan Britain.

CHAPTER FOUR
CORINEUS

Cornwall: a land steeped in myths, legend and mystery, a land fiercely proud of its heritage. Craggy mist-shrouded sea cliffs and spooky desolate moors have been the backbone of smuggling pirates and red-eyed monsters in folklore and literature throughout the ages. Works by greats such as Sir Arthur Conan Doyle and Robert Louis Stevenson have all woven tales of adventure and intrigue in the most westerly county of England.

It is not surprising that with such a rich tapestry of folklore and stunning scenery Cornwall is still considered by many to be the home of myth and legend in the United Kingdom. Everyone I know who walks a Pagan path is in love with Kernow (the Cornish word for Cornwall). I have to admit that I haven't spent that much time in that neck of the woods even though I live in Somerset, just down the road. It is something that I intend to remedy in the future.

So who is this Corineus fellow? I must confess that while researching this book I came across characters that I had never heard of before and Corineus is one of them. Corineus, in medieval British legend, was a prodigious warrior, a superhero for the British people, a slayer of giants, and the heroic founder of Cornwall itself.

According to the great chronicler Geoffrey of Monmouth we have some information regarding the history of Corineus. In Monmouth's *History of the Kings of Britain* (1136) we are told that he was the leader of the descendants of the Trojans who had fled with Antenor sometime after the Trojan War and settled on the coasts of the Tyrrhenian Sea. We then skip to a character named Brutus who we are told was a descendant of the Trojan Prince Aeneas. Having been exiled from Italy and liberating the enslaved Trojans in Greece, he encountered Corineus and his people, who subsequently joined him in his travels. It would appear that they made for a formidable team. It is then calmly explained that whilst in Gaul, Corineus provoked a war with Goffarius Pictus, King of Aquitania, by hunting in his forests without permission! It would appear that Corineus wasn't really bothered about the rules regarding hunting and was happy to engage in the true "outlaw" pastime of poaching. It goes on to tell us that in the ensuing war he was responsible for killing thousands single-handedly with his battle-axe. After defeating Goffarius, the Trojans decided to cross the English Channel to the mysterious island of Albion, which Brutus ceremoniously renamed Britain, after himself. Corineus decided to settle in Cornwall, which at this time was inhabited by anti-social and aggressive giants. Within a short space of time Brutus and his army had managed to kill most of them, but their leader, Gogmagog, was kept alive for the specific reason of having a wrestling match with Corineus. It was stated that Gogmagog stood twelve feet tall and was so strong that he would uproot oak trees as if they were a hazel wand! Wow, this man must have been some kind of warrior to accept a fight with the leader of the giants! A footnote to this would be the fact that even to this day there is a strong tradition of Cornish Wrestling. Evidence of this can be seen at fairs and folk gatherings throughout the year and at locations all around the county. I really do admire the Cornish folk who still hold on to their traditions and way of life. Have a look on the 'net for yourself;

it is rather interesting. The fight itself is said to of taken place near Plymouth, located in modern day Devon, but conflicting information states that the location of the match was really Totnes in Devon which is named Giant's Leap to this day. Personally I have my doubts on both locations due to the geographical locations. I understand that Cornwall was bigger then and its boundaries were within modern day Devon but I would have thought that if the tale was in fact true, the site of this epic battle would have been further into Cornwall itself. Having said that, the history books tell us that when Brutus and Corineus made landfall it was at Totnes; presumably they had made their way up the River Dart. Of course this is mere conjecture and speculation on my part for we don't even know if there is any historical basis for the story. We are told that Corineus was victorious and defeated the giant by throwing him over a cliff, hence the name Giant's Leap, although that name would suggest Gogmagog intentionally and voluntarily threw himself over the precipice.

Corineus is cited as the first of the legendary rulers of Cornwall and as with all good tales of royalty, the skulduggery didn't take long to begin to rear its ugly head. After his cohort Brutus died, the rest of Britain was divided between his three sons, Locrinus (England), Kamber (Wales) and Albanactus (Scotland). Locrinus had agreed to marry Corineus' daughter Gwendolen, but instead had fallen in love with Estrildis, a captured German princess. Corineus threatened war in response to this affront, and to pacify him Locrinus married Gwendolen, but kept Estrildis as his secret mistress. After Corineus died, Locrinus divorced Gwendolen and married Estrildis, and Gwendolen responded by raising an army in Cornwall and declaring war against her ex-husband. It would appear that Gwendolen had inherited her father's forthright approach to problem-solving. As a result of the conflict it is said that Gwendolen was victorious and that Locrinus was killed during the battle, but still not amused by her ex-husband's actions and honour not satisfied, Gwendolen proceeded to throw Estrildis and her daughter, Habren, into the River Severn!

When you see the rugged landscape of Cornwall one can see how it inspires tales of epic battles and magical heroes. Maybe Dartmoor (an area of vast moorland just North West of Totnes) and its huge

Tor rock formations were the inspiration for the tales of giants. I know in Iceland and other Northern European countries folklore states that huge rock formations are indeed giants or trolls turned to stone aeons before the modern time. In my opinion, there might have been a Corineus and he was most likely the first "recorded" King of Cornwall; however, I very much doubt he fought giants and laid waste to thousands with his awe-inspiring battle axe! Of course propaganda is a powerful tool and centuries ago the spoken word was the email and YouTube of the day. Travellers roamed the known world whispering tales of heroic feats and I would suggest within a few years word of his stature had spread. As with most stories, it gets embellished and added to the more people recant it. The first man states his friend caught a two-foot fish; by the fiftieth person it was a man-eating whale, thirty feet long with teeth the size of a man! Ok, maybe that's a bit of an exaggeration but you get the point.

Whatever you believe is entirely your choice; was he real or a mere fantasy? Was he just an ordinary man or a true colossus amongst lesser folk? Whichever way you decide there is no doubt that his legend still enthrals us to this day and for the true Cornishman, Corineus was—and still is—a Pagan hero.

CHAPTER FIVE
CÚ CHULAINN

In this chapter we begin by winging our way over the Irish Sea to the Emerald Isle. I love Ireland and its link to its ancient past. Rolling hills and stunning scenery make it an idyllic setting for fairy tales and folklore; it has become in recent years the location of choice for sweeping epics bound for the silver screen. The popular television show *Game of Thrones* is filmed there as was the 2004 movie *King Arthur*, so it stands to reason that such a glorious country would have its fair share of Pagan superheroes, would it not? And that it does.

Cú Chulainn: a name synonymous with masculinity and heroic virtue, a true champion of Ireland. However, he was not just limited to Ireland; his exploits are also a mainstay across the waters of western Britain and feature as a titan in Scottish and Manx folklore. Cú Chulainn, Irish for "Culann's Hound" and sometimes known in English as Cuhullin, is an Irish mythological hero who appears in the stories and sagas of the *Ulster Cycle*. The

Ulster Cycle,(formerly known as the *Red Branch Cycle*) is one of the four great cycles of Irish mythology. It is a volume of medieval Irish heroic legends and sagas of the traditional heroes of the Ulaid in what is now eastern Ulster and northern Leinster, particularly counties Armagh, Down and Louth, and taking place around or before the 1st century AD. As we can see, our hero certainly has some pedigree because not only was he a great warrior but he was the son of the God Lugh. His original name was Sétanta but he gained his historical name after he killed Culann's ferocious guard dog in self-defence and offered his services as a substitute until a permanent replacement could be found. Of course this was pretty impressive for a young man but this just the mere start of a career steeped in fantasy.

In the mythology surrounding our hero it is at the age of seventeen that he is reported to have single-handedly defended Ulster against the armies of Medb, Queen of Connacht in the epic Táin Bó Cúailnge ("Cattle Raid of Cooley"). Due to his resounding martial successes, the spiritual leaders at that time prophesied that his great deeds of valour would give him everlasting fame. However, there was to be a price for such immortality—his life was destined to be a short one. Among his attributes it is said that he possessed battle-frenzy, or "ríastrad— translated as "warp spasm"— in which he becomes an unrecognisable, indestructible monster who knows neither friend nor foe and lays waste to everyone and everything around him. It would appear that this ability is akin to the Bezerker in Viking lore, warriors who were the epitome of brutality even by Dark Age standards. Some believe that a cocktail of shamanic workings, magical rituals, alcohol and even hallucinogenic mushrooms propelled the warrior into a blood lust. Some have argued that they did not use magic mushrooms; however, I myself am an ardent advocate for the theory.

Unlike most on our valiant list he is renowned for using cutting-edge weaponry and a more elaborate form of transport. It is said he fought from his chariot, driven by his loyal charioteer Láeg and drawn by his horses, Liath Macha and Dub Sainglend. Of course anyone with any sort of Heathen interest would notice the similarities between him and the Norse God Thor, who also rides a chariot. Could there be a connection? Does it all stem from the same folklore, then evolve individually due to geographical location? Food for thought, I believe. It is also relevant (whilst talking about similarities) that Cú Chulainn shows striking resemblance to the Persian epic hero Rostam, as well as to the Germanic Lay of Hildebrand and even the trials and tribulations of the Greek hero Hercules. Could this add credence to my hypothesis suggesting a common Indo-European origin link? Without archaeological evidence we will never know.

As we journey through his youth it is remarked that even though he is a good-looking chap, Cú Chulainn is still single and hasn't found a wife. Due to his abilities it is said that this terrified the local men, for they feared he would use his strength to steal their own wives and daughters and they would powerless to stop such a mighty warrior. They decided to search the length and breadth of the land but to no avail, for Cú Chulainn had made his choice and would not bend to the will of those who opposed it. Enter our beautiful heroine: Emer, the daughter of Forgall Monach. She was captivating and the one our hero desired more than any other. Unfortunately her father opposed the union and knowing what a man our hero was, formulated a cunning plan. He suggested that Cú Chulainn should train in martial arts and arms with the renowned and reclusive warrior-woman Scáthach (more of her in a latter chapter) across the water in the land of Alba (Scotland). Of course we immediately see this plan for what it is and Forgall is confident that Cú Chulainn will either refuse or disappear forever and very probably be killed. As far as Forgall was concerned, it was a no-lose situation. It would seem, however, that Forgall underestimated the would-be suitor and Cú Chulainn took up the challenge, traveling to her residence Dún Scáith (Fortress of Shadows) on the Isle of Skye. Incidentally, the mountain ranges on the Isle of Skye are called the Cuillin Mountains, reportedly named after our Irish friend. I have spent a lot of time on Skye and can honestly say it is breathtaking, if you ever get a chance to go, do so; you will love it. I never did find the Fortress of Shadows, though.

Meanwhile, back home Forgall offers Emer to another, whom after discovering her love for the mighty Cú Chulainn rejects the offer. He had good reason to be scared for whilst this was happening our hero had defied the odds and was in the process of being taught the mysteries of war by a woman who would make most men run for cover!

We don't really know the time frame but what we do know is that Scáthach taught Cú Chulainn all the arts of war, including the use of the Gáe Bulg, a pain-inducing barbed spear, which is thrown with the foot and has to be cut out of its victim.

During his time on Skye we are told that he is not the only one being trained by Scáthach. His fellow trainees include Ferdiad, who becomes Cú Chulainn's best friend and foster-brother. Where exactly all these other trainees come from is a mystery but we do know that only Cú Chulainn is trained in the super scary spear of pain!

During his time on Skye there are many ups and downs, the most notable being the rivalry between his teacher and another. Scáthach faces a battle against Aífe, her most feared rival (some say it is actually her twin sister, others have hypothesised that it is a metaphor for an inner turmoil regarding her sexual feelings for her charge). We do know that she fears Aífe's prowess on the battlefield. It spurs her to drug Cú Chulainn but due to his immense strength it only has an effect for one hour. As soon as he wakes up he leaps into the fray. We are informed that in single combat they are both evenly matched and the fight shows no sign of a victor until our hero distracts her and forces her to the ground. In true hero fashion he spares her life in exchange for a truce with her "sister" and that she bear him a child, specifically a son. I am convinced that if this tale were true that it was Scáthach all along and it was she who bore the son. But that is just my humble opinion. Leaving Aífe pregnant, Cú Chulainn sets off from Scotland fully trained and returns home, but after successfully completing the challenge set to him Forgall still refuses to let him marry Emer. Cú Chulainn is at this point rather livid and decides to storm Forgall's fortress and in the process kills twenty-four of Forgall's warriors. He then adds insult to injury when he abducts Emer and steals Forgall's treasure. It is said that Forgall himself falls from the ramparts to his death. The legend doesn't say specifically that he commits suicide but I would wager after taking such a humiliating beating it is highly probable.

CHAPTER SIX
HENGEST AND HORSA

When we sift our way through the heroes of these fair lands we can't help but be drawn back yet again to the vast array of heroes arising from the Anglo Saxon period. As I have already mentioned in this book and my previous work, the Anglo Saxon mind-set was well rooted within the warrior/hero aspect, and in fact was such an integral part of their psyche as well as the building blocks for the stuff of legends.

According to ancient English tales the Germanic brothers Hengest and Horsa (the Old English names Hengest and Horsa mean "stallion" and "horse" respectively)arrived in Britain as Anglo Saxon mercenaries in the employ of Vortigern, King of the Britons to help against the Picts between AD 446 and 454. Early chroniclers stated that the brothers were indeed the sons of the God Woden (Woden being the Anglo Saxon equivalent of the Norse God Odin).It is universally agreed upon that this event heralded the beginning of the Anglo-Saxon "invasion" of Britain. Although in modern times the term "invasion" would imply thousands of soldiers, I believe it wasn't that dramatic. In my opinion it would have happened in drips and drabs and over a longer period of time as some modern historians are now suggesting. We can't know for sure, so as always we must formulate our own opinions regarding the extent of the "invasion". I would be more inclined to call it the Anglo Saxon expansion.

It would appear that all was well for a time and the brothers were making quite the name for themselves as warriors, amassing wealth and renown. They fought many campaigns under the banner of Vortigern, against not only rival Britons but also the Welsh. However, the good times were not to last. After a few years' faithful service of being the King's royal "bad asses" we get a glimpse of the apparent ruthlessness and ambition of the brothers. It is in the writing *Historia Brittonum* that we are introduced to the idea that Hengest had an unnamed daughter who reputedly seduced King Vortigern, thus being the catalyst for what is known as the Treachery of the Long Knives in which Hengest's men butchered and massacred the Britons whilst at a peace accord. Some may suggest it was a premeditated move to obtain power and to use as a prerequisite to war; some hypothesise it was merely a young woman who fell in love and it all went a bit pear-shaped! That fact that Hengest had ordered his men to hide blades under their feet and that they draw said weapons when he cried "*nima der sexa*" (take out the sword) should in no way be misconstrued! Some early sources indicate and give hints to the theory that the other brother, Horsa, died fighting during the battle with the Britons. However, the fate of Hengest is unclear. No details are provided regarding his death until Geoffrey's *Historia*, which states that Hengest was in fact beheaded by Eldol, the British Duke of Gloucester, and then buried in a nondescript mound, the location of which is unknown.

Whatever happened and regardless of conflicting tales, we can't deny the impact of the brothers within the Anglo Saxon world and their legacy left for us to ponder. It is interesting to note that a figure named Hengest who in my opinion is in fact the leader of British legend or a representation of, appears in the *Finnesburg Fragment* and in the Anglo Saxon masterpiece, *Beowulf*. It is also interesting to note that such was the allure of the brothers' legend that subsequent kings of Kent stated they could trace their bloodline directly back to Hengest, one would presume to add gravitas to their reign and military prowess. But it is not just during this period of history that their names are spoken or used with enduring passion. In what is now known as present-day Northern Germany, and up until the late 19th century, horse head gables, or gable signs adorned with two rampant horse figures were referred to as "Hengest and Hors", a fascinating ode to Germanic heroes.

Throughout many tribal peoples of Northern Europe there are many founding horse-associated brother myths and legends, and interestingly they also appear in other Indo-European cultures. Of course with such a wide populace and similarities regarding the brothers, this has inevitably sparked debate within the folklore/historic community and scholars have theorized a pan-Germanic mythological origin for Hengest and Horsa, specifically stemming from divine twins found in Proto-Indo-European religion. This as a theory makes sense to me; however, you might surmise your own theory regarding the origins of the myths surrounding the brothers. I'm sure we can find similarities in faiths across the world; one just has to look at the similarities between Babylonian/Sumerian lore and that of Christianity. With such a back story it is not surprising that they have had some rather impressive advocates, for example, the scholar J. R. R. Tolkien (amongst others) has argued a historical basis for Hengest and Horsa and even used them as a basis for his literary characters. In modern times the brothers are still used by many Nationalistic folk as "the Fathers of England" due to the fact that the natives were called Britons and they were the initial instigators of the Anglo Saxon/Jutish era in these fair lands, hence the start of the island being called England. It is also interesting that in Maidstone, Kent there is a stone known as the White Horse stone that happens to feature in the historical accounts of Hengest and Horsa. Legend says when Horsa died Hengest raised a monument in his memory. According to myth, the White Horse Stone is the traditional site, and may actually have been where Horsa was buried although I know of no evidence to support this theory. The site itself remains a very important place not just for those of an Anglo Saxon Heathenry path but of anyone who is proud to be called English.

Again, what you believe is completely your own affair. I personally believe there is sufficient evidence to prove beyond reasonable doubt that they did in fact exist and that they arrived on these shores as paid mercenaries in the service of the Briton King. I am left with little doubt that they were incredibly skilled warriors who dominated the battlefield, thus leaving us tales of adventure and an everlasting sense of national pride when their names are spoken. But they are not the only heroes to arise from such a turbulent and bloodthirsty time. Years later a warrior took up the sword in defence of these shores, a warrior that I personally have a soft spot for, a Guerrilla fighter taking the war to the enemy and leaving a bloody trail across the east of England. His name was Hereward the Wake.

CHAPTER SEVEN
HEREWARD THE WAKE

When I started to research Hereward the Wake I was convinced that he was indeed a Pagan. As it turns out, I could be mistaken! However, in my defence he is of such importance as a heroic hero within English history I could not help myself for including him in such a book. I also feel, because he was named a "terrorist" by William the Conqueror thus being a "devil" in Christian eyes, one could argue that he indeed becomes a Pagan hero by default.

Hereward the Wake (also known as Hereward the Outlaw or Hereward the Exile, (c. 1035 – c.1072) was an 11th-century leader of local resistance to the Norman conquest of England. It is said that Hereward's base, when leading the rebellion against the Norman rulers, was located in the areas that cover the Isle of Ely. It is also rumoured that he and his rebellious band of outlaws roamed the Fens, covering modern day North Cambridgeshire, Southern Lincolnshire and West Norfolk. According to legend he sulked in the shadows, whipping up opposition to William the Conqueror and all of his supporters.

It is interesting that when we take an in-depth look at one's birth name we can perhaps catch a glimpse of the said person's future. In this case Hereward is an Old English name, composed of the elements here "army" and weard "guard" (cognate with the Old High German name Heriwart).The epithet "the Wake" is recorded in the late 14th century, and may mean "the watchful", or derive from the Anglo-Norman Wake family who later claimed descent from him. Of course this could be merely coincidental; I will leave it up to you to draw your own conclusion.

As with so much in history, the origins of Hereward are surrounded with mystery and smoke. As time-explorers all we can do is sift the few fragments left behind from scholars and folklore. Partly because of the sketchiness and lack of evidence for his existence, his life has become a magnet for a vast amount of speculation and more than a handful of theories regarding his true lineage. The earliest references to his parentage is said that he is the son of Edith, a descendent of Oslac of York and

Leofric of Bourne, nephew of Ralph the Staller. However a conflicting standpoint has suggested that Leofric, Earl of Mercia and his wife Lady Godiva were in fact Hereward's real parents. I am sceptical of this hypothesis as there is no supportive evidence for this. Also, Abbot Brand of Peterborough who was reportedly Hereward's uncle does not appear to have been related to either Leofric or Godiva. I find it strange that if Hereward were a member of this prominent family – his parentage would not only be a matter of public record but also a family title worthy of praise even in today's modern world. In recent times some modern researchers have suggested him to have been Anglo-Danish with a Danish father, Asketil; since Brand is also a Danish name, it stands to reason that the Abbot may have in fact been Asketil's brother. Hereward's apparent ability to call on Danish support seems entirely plausible, thus adding credence and support to this theory.

Within modern history Hereward's birth is generally dated as 1035/6 due to written works of that time indicate that he was first exiled in 1054, in his 18th year. However, we must remain analytical and sceptical when reading such works as I believe that as the myth of Hereward evolved over the years, so did his mystique and that scholars inflated the tales as time passed. Thus many modern day scholars lean to the side that most of his early life may have been exaggerated. Of course this is not an isolated phenomenon; I wager every great historical figure has had some sort of embellishment thrust upon their legacy. It is stated that his place of birth was in or in the vicinity of Bourne in Lincolnshire. To add weight to such a statement that great work of medieval taxation *The Domes day Book* states that a man named Hereward held lands in the parishes of Witham on the Hill and Barholm with Stow in the south-western corner of Lincolnshire as a tenant of Peterborough Abbey. It also tells us that prior to his exile Hereward had also held lands as a tenant of Croyland Abbey at Crowland, eight miles east of Market Deeping in the neighbouring fenland. Of course we have to remind ourselves that In those times it was a marshy and unpleasant area and since the holdings of abbeys could be widely dispersed across parishes, the precise location of his personal holdings is uncertain but was certainly somewhere in modern day south Lincolnshire.

Now we get to the good stuff, the start of his adventures and why I included him in this book. According to the *Gesta Hereward* (a medieval book written at this time) Hereward was banished and exiled at the tender age of eighteen for generally being a scallywag, disobedience to his father and disruptive behaviour, which was causing problems among the local community and no doubt bringing "shame" on his household. He was also declared an outlaw by Edward the Confessor. It doesn't really explain why he was deemed an outlaw but it must have been for something a little more serious than refusing to tidy his room! The Gesta recounts many stories of his supposed adventures as a fresh-faced young man while in exile in Cornwall, Ireland and Flanders. These include a fight with an enormous bear and the rescue of a Cornish princess from an unwanted marriage! Although these seem amazing many historians without a sense of humour nor imagination deem these tales to be largely fictions; of course I say, "To hell with them!" Who hasn't wrestled a bear in their youthful days? Now fast forward a few years to 1066, to the time of the Norman invasion of England. Legend states he was still in exile in Europe, working as a successful mercenary for Baldwin V. At this point most historians seem to agree that tales of him falling in love, taking part in tournaments and living the high life are largely correct; however, these carefree days did last and bad news from Blighty galvanized him in action.

It is said Hereward returned to England in late 1069 or 1070. Upon his arrival, he discovered that his family's lands had been plundered and laid claim to by the Normans and his brother had been brutally killed, culminating with his head being stuck on a spike at the gate to his house! Of course Hereward was not amused by such actions and swiftly took revenge on the Normans who killed his brother while they were ridiculing the English at a drunken feast. Folklore tells us that in true outlaw fashion he engaged all of them in combat and allegedly killed fifteen of them with the assistance of only one helper. Wow, he must have been one hell of a fighter if this were indeed true. The one helper must have been the "getaway driver". After dispatching said gaggle of bad guys he then gathered followers and went to Peterborough Abbey to be knighted by his uncle Abbot Brand. He then did a sensible thing and did a runner by returning briefly to Flanders, presumably to allow the situation to cool down before returning to England once again.

During this time period, in or around 1070, it is said that Hereward participated in what he is most famous for: the anti-Norman insurrection centred on the Isle of Ely. In 1070 the Danish king Sweyn Estrithson sent a small army to try to establish a camp on the Isle of Ely. It would appear that Hereward joined them, then led the contingent, thus ending up storming and sacking Peterborough Abbey not just with the Danes but also with a growing number of local men rallying to the outlaw's cause. There is conflicting information regarding this siege; while the Gesta says this was after the main battle at Ely, the Peterborough Chronicle says it was before. The historical consensus is that the Chronicle's account is most accurate. I find it somewhat amusing that Hereward's apparent reasoning and self-justification behind the attack was said to have been that he wished to save the Abbey's treasures and relics from the rapacious Normans led by the new Norman abbot who had ousted his Uncle Brand! Whether or not you buy into such a tall tale or err on the side of plausibility you can't help but admire his resolve! As with much of this tale we are presented yet more conflicting evidence. According to the Gesta he returned the treasures looted from the abbey after having a vision of Saint Peter. However, the Peterborough Chronicle says that the treasures disappeared to Denmark! Personally I am more inclined to believe that the treasures found their way across the water and made some Danes rather happy, as opposed to Christian propaganda and yet more hijacking of Anglo Saxon heroes!

After all this, Hereward was then joined by a small but battle-hardened army led by the Saxon Morcar, the former Earl of Northumbria who had been unjustly ousted by William. In true Norman prowess, William sent an army to deal with the rebels. In 1071, Hereward and Morcar were forced to retreat to their stronghold based deep within the Fens and made a defiant stand on the Isle of Ely against the Conqueror's rule. It is interesting that both the *Gesta Herewardi* and the *Liber Eliensis* claim that the Normans made a frontal assault. Of course the Normans were used to head-on battles as opposed to Hereward's guerrilla tactics but in this case it was not to help the Normans' cause. Their attack on the stronghold was dependant on a huge, mile-long timber causeway, but predictably this sank under the weight of armour and horses. The Normans then tried to intimidate the English with a witch, who cursed them from a wooden tower. Of course you would think that I would cheer for the witch due to her being a Pagan, but I have a soft spot for Hereward. In true heroic fashion, Hereward managed to set a fire that toppled the tower with the witch in it, thus adding more fuel to the fire that was Hereward's mythical status.

The books then tell us that the Normans, most probably led by one of William's knights named Belasius, then crossed the land with gold and bribed the monks of the island to reveal a safe route across the marshes, resulting in Ely's capture. Boo! I hear you cry. The defiant Morcar was captured and imprisoned, but what of our hero? Hereward is said to have escaped with some of his ardent followers and fled into the wild fenland to have continued his resistance against the invading force. For once we can relax and trust this information as it seems his escape is noted in all the earliest surviving sources, thus making it as accurate as we can possibly get.

So I know you are still not convinced on why I included a Christian hero fighting other Christians in a Pagan book. Well my friend, the truth of the matter is this: I respect the man. As far as I can tell he fought for nothing more than to free his people from an oppressive ruling class hell-bent on subjugating the indigenous population, a man who left title and privilege behind to take up the sword and stand up for the little people. I respect such actions even if it comes from a man of another faith or religion. We are our deeds not our words. I believe that these are true Pagan traits and ones that I personally hold dear. Was he a Pagan in the truest sense of the word? No. But I do believe he has earned the right to be an honorary one through his actions. It could also be said that he was deemed an enemy of the Church, so by definition he was "evil". As we all know Pagans are also classed as evil, thus joining him and us in hell-bound unison. Food for thought.

CHAPTER EIGHT
HERNE THE HUNTER

I think it is safe to say that within every Earth-based spiritual path there is always a reference to a forest-dwelling man who lives deep within the wooded realm. This figure is usually a teacher whose job it is to instruct those of the path to rejoice in nature and to gain strength from the ancient knowledge that flows through its very being. We have all heard of the term "Mother Earth" and as far as I am concerned the Ying Yang paradigm insists that a male force be present, hence the personification of the "Man of the Forest". Throughout the world this figure has many names but for this chapter I shall only use the one relevant to the Pagan/Anglo Saxon Britons. Of course there have been many books written specifically about this figure but I am happy to lend my thoughts to a single chapter.

I first became aware of this masculine energy when, as a young boy in 1984, I was introduced to the television program *Robin of Sherwood*. Of course I admit I had no idea of the impact this figure would have on my life in my later years, but at the time I remember being mesmerised by this powerful figure, his head adorned with stag horns. Of course this figure had a name, Herne the Hunter, but this meant nothing to a boy of nine staring intently at Robin Hood and his band of outlaws! If you have ever seen this TV show then you will understand just how "Pagan" the show is. In later years when I watched it again I was truly amazed at the imagery and Pagan-specific dialogue scripted within the show and how well they wove Anglo Saxon folklore and legend into another generic telling of a well-known tale. As we know Herne was a major force in helping Robin became "The Hooded Man", a force of rebellion against a tyrannical king (but more on him later).

But what do we really know about this Herne chap? To be honest—not a lot; in fact there is not much recorded history about him until the 1840s, made by none other than William Shakespeare. We must remember when I say "no history" I am of course referring to modern historically accounts in mainstream literature as opposed to hundreds of years' worth of oral evidence regarding the "Green

Man", etc. But for now let's just concentrate on the actual name Herne. It is stated by Mr Shakespeare that Herne is a spiritual/magical entity whose job it is to safeguard Windsor forest. He also tells us that during the winter months he can be seen dancing and skulking around an oak tree, stag antlers upon his head. It is interesting that some have said he was banished for a wrongdoing and couldn't bear the shame, thus hanging himself from a tree, forever wandering the forest in limbo. This spiritual apparition is said to collect other huntsman souls along his way and tales of hauntings regarding Herne and his like still surface today around the Berkshire/Hampshire/Surrey areas. Others claim they have witnessed his appearance accompanied by demon hounds and a horned owl! Yet others claim he was nothing more than an aristocrat. Over the years there have been many a theory put forward regarding Herne yet none have shown any real tangible evidence regarding his origins.

When we delve deeper into the theory of Herne hanging himself it gets a little more tangled. The supposed location of his demise known locally as Herne's Oak was, for many years, a matter of local speculation and controversy. It is said some ordnance survey maps show Herne's Oak a little to the north of Frogmore House in the Home Park (adjoining Windsor Great Park). This is generally believed to be the correct site from which the oak of Shakespeare's time was felled in 1796. Of course this is not to say the Bard was indeed correct and there is always at least one person who wants to upset the applecart. For example in 1838, Edward Jesse claimed that a different tree in the avenue was in fact the real Herne's Oak, and his theory gained popularity especially with none other than Queen Victoria herself. As a parting note this tree was blown down on 31 August 1863, and Queen Victoria ordered another tree planted on the exact site but this tree was removed in 1906 when the avenue was replanted once again.

Many scholars over the years have made the link that Herne is in fact a lot older than modern day historians believe. Many believe that "Herne" as well as other wild huntsmen in European folklore all derive from the same ancient source—that of the Gaulish deity known as Cernunnos. Some have suggested that the word "horns" is a cognate of the Latin word "cornu", and this seems to me to be highly plausible. However when we look further we find that evidence for the worship of Cernunnos has only been recovered from the European mainland, and not in Britain. At first glance some would say this is problematic when we attempt to link the two but there are other glimpses of information that connect the fragments. While scholars argue over the mainland Europe conundrum back here in the UK and specifically the Anglo Saxon period In the Early Middle Ages, we know that Windsor Forest fell under the control of the Pagan Angles who worshiped their own pantheon of gods, including their chief God Woden, who has sometimes been depicted as horned. Is it possible that Herne is in fact a depiction of Woden? Or of the Norse version Odin who was known to ride across the night sky with his own Wild Hunt and who interestingly also hung himself on the world tree known as Yggdrasil to learn the secrets of the runes? I fancy the similarities are too many to discard.

Truth is, we honestly don't know where he came from or from what culture he belongs. I however believe that as a Heathen/Pagan living in the UK I must acknowledge that Herne or at least, the "essence" of Herne plays a big role within my spirituality. In my opinion there is too much emphasis placed on the "feminine" aspect within modern day Paganism. Some I have encountered have even discarded the masculine altogether! This to me is nonsensical as we have to have balance. Whether you see him as Herne or Cernunnos or something else entirely you have to accept the fact that Herne represents the masculine energy within all of us. He is the hunter, the protector and the wisdom from the woods. Do I believe he is a Pagan hero? Without a doubt, for he is the one that gives ME the power to stand up for what I believe is right. A lesson we all need to learn.

CHAPTER NINE
JACK THE GIANT KILLER

Violence, graphic scenes of blood and gore—what more do you want from a heroic tale to fire the imagination! Cornwall has always been associated with big, brutish giants smashing and splatting their way to dominance for thousands of years; in fact, nearly all the tales of giants within British folklore originate from the most westerly part of the UK. Although there are tales of these gigantic foes throughout this mighty land, we will concentrate our attention to the place I call home, the South West of England.

Unless you are from that neck of the woods, extremely well up on your folklore or have seen the recent Hollywood movie you may not have heard of our next hero. To be honest I didn't really know much about him and after doing my research found that I could write an entire book on this character alone. Again, like my other chapters I shall just give a basic overview and encourage the reader to explore for himself or herself, should they wish to do so.

Jack the Giant Killer is a Cornish/British fairy tale and legend cantered on a rather happy-go-lucky lad who spends his time wandering around the West Country slaying a number of giants for fun. We are informed that this tale is set during King Arthur's reign. Of course since we don't even know for sure about King Arthur we can't really say when this is set with any real certainty. As with many legends within British folklore pinning down a specific time period and geographical area is hazy at best and becomes a contentious issue among those trawling through history. With this in mind it is not unusual to find that neither Jack nor his tale of high adventure are referenced in English literature prior to the eighteenth century, and his story only appeared in print for the first time in 1711. There are those that explain this late arrival by way of saying that people had grown weary and somewhat bored of King Arthur "the greatest of all giant killers", thus Jack was created as a new literary hero whose role was to be the killer of giants and a worthy replacement for Arthur. Also it is worth pointing out the similarities with tales from

Northern Scandinavian folk lore, specifically the God Thor's run-in with the giant Skrymir, which bares more than a likeness to Jack's encounter.

The United Kingdom has had a rich fascination with giants throughout its history, both orally and in the written word; in fact, one can still see these giants in the modern age. The author John Matthews writes in his book, *Taliesin, Shamanism and the Bardic Mysteries of Britain and Ireland (*1992) that giants are extremely prevalent throughout British folklore, and in his opinion represent the "original" inhabitants, ancestors, or gods of the island before the coming of "civilised man", their imposing stature a visual clue regarding their "otherworldly" and "superior" prowess, thus adding gravitas to their lore. One such example that remains to this day is the Cerne Abbas Giant. Some believe it represents a giant whilst others disagree; however, regardless of the true meaning it is a visual delight and has the power to stir one's imagination. What we do now about the Cerne Abbas Giant is that it is a hill figure near the village of Cerne Abbas in Dorset, England. Made by a turf-cut outline filled with chalk, it depicts a large, naked man, with a rather large erect penis, typically described as a giant wielding a club. I am happy to report that the figure is listed as a scheduled monument in the United Kingdom; thus, the site where he stands is owned by the National Trust, safeguarding its presence for future generations.

Throughout the years the figure has been the subject of much study and speculation, but in truth its origin and age still remain a mystery. It is often thought of as an ancient construction; however the earliest mention of it dates to the late 17th century, obviously a little too "modern" to be classed as an ancient monument. Early scholars associated it with a Saxon deity, while other scholars sought to identify it with a Celtic British figure or the Roman Hercules, or some blending of the two. Again, with very little evidence it would be a stretch to date it from these periods. Archaeological evidence might suggest that parts of the drawing have been lost over time and may strengthen the Hercules identification but once again the lack of earlier descriptions leads modern day time-investigators to conclude that it may date from the 17th century and some also go as far as to say it is some sort of political satire. However, regardless of its age or origins the fact remains that the Cerne Abbas Giant has become an important part of local culture and folklore, and has woven itself into the very fabric of modern day culture. Even to this day many associate it with fertility and the power of masculinity, which seems a bit obvious considering the size of its colossal todger! Regardless of your personal opinion regarding its origins it has cemented itself as one of England's best known hill figures and is a major visitor attraction in the region.

Whilst I was conducting research I was amazed about the wealth of material regarding Jack but in truth could not find much of any real substance that would be concise enough to add to this chapter. It became painfully obvious that I could write a hundred more pages spouting quote after quote about theories regarding this hero but in truth I feel I would be doing, you, the reader an injustice. It is not my intention to write the "definitive" guide to Pagan heroes nor an academically accurate study regarding the merits of historical presumptions or evidence. This has been the most difficult chapter to write thus far and I have tried to give you a little information regarding Jack and his tales of giant-smashing but as I delved deeper into the myths the more I found it interwoven with many others tales (some even linked to others within this book). I decided to leave this chapter where it is and as always encourage you to investigate should your curiosity be tingling. As with every challenge in life every cloud has a silver lining and the upside to hitting this particular brick wall whilst writing is that whilst researching Jack I found myself on a journey, a spider's web if you like of interconnecting myths and folklore that sent me into uncharted territory regarding the ancient beliefs of this land. It has fired my imagination and filled me with purpose to investigate these new deities and characters from our distant past. In truth, a lot of these avenues revealed new ideas for future books. When I start a new book I always try to write some sort of "story arc" so I know where I am heading and at which point in the book. However, sometimes it goes a little off-kilter, so forgive me if I have digressed and let us move on to our next hero, a hero who needs no other introduction but his name, the King of the Britons, the defender of all that is mighty and the historical guardian of all that is right. Ladies and Gentlemen, I give you King Arthur.

HEROES OF PAGAN BRITAIN

CHAPTER TEN
KING ARTHUR

I challenge anyone in the UK to say her or she has never heard of King Arthur. From comics and modern literature to television and epic movies, King Arthur has been at the forefront of our collective imaginations for decades. Pagan or not, his name is synonymous with "Great Britain"—but there is a catch. With all this pro-Arthur propaganda you would have thought that we would have concrete evidence of his life and unequivocal proof he was real, but alas, this couldn't be further from the truth. For all our bluster and flag-waving there is no tangible evidence to say that he even existed at all. But how come he is so well-known, I hear you cry. That, my friends, is a question that we shall try to answer. In fact, I have my own theories to why our culture has latched onto this hero and why he means so much to the Anglo Britons. It started many years ago when we as a country were struggling for an Identity. But before I give you my thoughts let us delve in to some of what we "think" we know regarding Arthur and some of the conflicting theories regarding his existence. At the end of the chapter you just might have your own ideas regarding his true identity.

Let us step back in time to the late 5th and early 6th centuries. King Arthur is apparently defending native Britons from those horrible invading Saxon scoundrels who are hell-bent on raping and pillaging our fine country. This all sounds like rather scary stuff but what do we have in the way of evidence? The extremely sparse historical evidence and background of Arthur is gathered from various sources, including the *Annales Cambriae, the Historia Brittonum*, and the writings of Gildas. Arthur's name also occurs in early poetic sources such as *Y Gododdin*. Even though his name appears in different texts we are not given any concrete background on our hero, only mere snippets of information. The legendary version of Arthur was developed as a figure of international interest largely through the popularity of that Dark Age media mogul Geoffrey of Monmouth and his rather fanciful and imaginative 12th-century work *Historia Regum Britanniae* (*History of the Kings of Britain*), from which it appears all tales were derived. We must also note that he was Christian so could it be possible that King Arthur was hijacked by Monmouth as a poster boy who was defending our "Christian" values from the "evil" "heathen" Saxons? But to do this one must presume that the native Britons were aware of a hero in their past named Arthur who protected them from danger. So is this proof in itself that Arthur did in fact exist and was of Pagan origins? It is also interesting that our mate Geoffrey not only depicted Arthur as the King of Britain who defeated the Saxons but as the King who established an empire over Britain, Ireland, Iceland, Norway and Gaul—the countries that just happened to be still in the "grip" of Pagan and Heathen subjugation. Call me paranoid but I find that a tad coincidental bordering on rather suspicious! Was Arthur being used as a Christian war hero to rally Europe against those who opposed Christianity? Of course I have no tangible proof to back up such a wild conspiracy theory but a lot more scholars and modern day truth-seekers are questioning the "normal" theories regarding our ancient past, especially when the only information we have comes from Christian scholars who had a personal faith-driven agenda to character assassinate those who they deemed "anti-Christian"

Of course the youth of today may only know of King Arthur from the BBC TV drama *Merlin.* Once again we can trace all these well-known characters and events such as Arthur's father Uther Pendragon, the wizard Merlin, Arthur's wife Guinevere, the sword Excalibur, Arthur's conception at Tintagel, his final battle against Mordred at Camlann, and final rest in Avalon to Geoffrey's *Historia*, all of which have a very "anti-" magical/Pagan connotation. Once again, maybe I am being a little too cynical to believe that it is some sort of anti-Pagan propaganda campaign but just because I am paranoid doesn't mean I am wrong! Of course there are other elements to the story that have been added to the famous tale we know today, for example the 12th-century French writer Chrétien de Troyes added Lancelot and the Holy Grail to the story thus beginning the familiar genre of Arthurian romance that became a significant and dominant mainstay of medieval literature. Interestingly in these French stories, the narrative focus often shifts from King Arthur himself to other characters, such as various Knights of the Round Table. Maybe the general public had become bored of the regurgitated tale and craved a little substance. Arthurian literature thrived during the middle Ages but for unknown reasons waned in the centuries that followed until it experienced a major resurgence in the 19th century and of course in the 21st century it has been widely explored in a vast era of artistic mediums.

When we are exploring a character from our distant past it stands to reason that the name itself should bear some sort of clue regarding the true origins of our quarry. For example, the prefix "Mac" in Scotland means "son of"; the "O" before a surname in Ireland means the same. Of course some names are regional-specific, thus illuminating the area for which the target of enquiry may have been born. However there are always those that will throw a spanner in the works regarding such investigation and some may even allude to a counter-argument regarding the origin of a name, calling into question our original thoughts because as we all know a name may sound very similar but may hail from entirely different locations, as is the case with the name Arthur. The origin of the Welsh name "Arthur" for example remains a matter of debate, even in modern times. Some have suggested that it is derived from the Roman family name Artorius. This has prompted some scholars to suggest that this is extremely relevant to this debate due to the legendary King Arthur's name only appears as Arthur, or Arturus, in early Latin Arthurian texts. To be honest there are so many theories regarding the origin of the name that we could be here for weeks and I am no expert on the languages used from which this evidence appears. Suffice to say that, once again we are left somewhat bamboozled regarding who is on the right track.

This really doesn't leave us with any real information or leads to which we may follow on our quest. So what about other elements from the legend that could help us identify our hero? You would have thought that location may shed some light on our quarry but alas once again every corner of the British Isles lays claim to the "fact" that King Arthur was born, died or resided in their location. There are the famous places that claim to be the site of a battle or in the case of Tintagel in Cornwall, the legendary Camelot itself. Of course Tintagel is not the only famous place to lay claim to the Arthurian legend, my own home town of Glastonbury is world-renowned for Arthur's grave, which resides in the grounds of Glastonbury Abbey. Most historians are somewhat sceptical of such a claim due to the fact that when the Abbey had a fire and was somewhat destitute and in need of funds a "miracle" occurred. The long-lost grave of Arthur and Guinevere was found in the grounds, thus creating a bit of a tourist draw which of course brought much needed revenue to the cash-strapped church! Even to this day it still has a magnetic effect on those seeking the resting place of Arthur. It also has to be mentioned that Glastonbury is sometimes called "Avalon" made famous by Arthurian tales. The Isle of Avalon is said to be a magical land, rising out of the mists. Although this may sound fanciful there could be an element of truth to this tale. Glastonbury itself is built on a hill with the Tor dominating the skyline on the Somerset levels. To the North are the Mendip Hills, to the West the Quantock Hills and the Black Down Hills are to the South. The Somerset levels are now marshland crisscrossed with droves that are a haven for wildlife and are there for the general public to enjoy; however, it was not always so. Many years ago the whole area was a flooded plane with pockets of people living on small parcels of land above the water line. One of the biggest recorded townships was that of Glastonbury and was only reachable by boat. As a traveller approaching Glastonbury and seeing the Tor rising from the mist and water line one could be forgiven for thinking it was in fact "Avalon". Combine this with the resident monk's flair for spinning a yarn you can see why it became a hub for folklore and legend. It is also worth mentioning that the monks themselves set up camp here due to the tale that Joseph of Arimathea visited the area and planted his staff into the ground, giving root to the Holy Thorn, a tree that is said not to grow anywhere else. The monks also claim that the abbey itself was started by Joseph at the wishes of Jesus.

I have my own theory to add to the mix. In a time when Paganism was still strong in the South West and possible tales of a Saxon hero saving the indigenous people would it not be prudent to capitalise on the Pagan propaganda surrounding the area, taking the basis of local belief and twisting it to your own religious worldview? If I was in charge of Glastonbury Abbey my first thought would be to rebrand a Pagan location as my own, then slowly twist local folklore into my own religious history. Could this explain the modern mix of Pagan and Christian lore associated to the same geographical location? Even today Glastonbury is world-famous not just for the Festival but as a hub for spiritual enlightenment regardless of faith practiced. Every week there seems to be a new celebration from another facet of new ageism. The Christians themselves have a festival in which they march through town and celebrate their faith. There is even a group who worship "The Goddess" whose name is "Nolava" which by pure coincidence is Avalon spelt backwards. I have to admit I know next to nothing about such a group but I am somewhat sceptical regarding the authenticity of such a faith; but at the end of the day who am I to judge.

Once again we are felt somewhat confused as to what to believe. Was he real or a mere character from legends passed down from our ancestors? Regardless of what our own personal views are there is no escaping the fact that King Arthur is synonymous with the British Isles and is part of the very fabric of folklore. His legacy remains into the modern age and still captivates our imaginations, from tales of his heroic deeds to the belief that he will once again rise to defend this land in its hour of dire need. The similarities between Arthur and other well-known defenders of justice are mere footnotes in the mists of history for we will never truly know from which his true self originates. During my research, yet again I was overwhelmed by the swath of theories and information regarding Britain's monarchic hero and when faced with such a deluge it was hard to cherry pick elements to include in this chapter. So as I draw to a close I would like to share my own personal view regarding the tale of King Arthur. I believe that Arthur did exist and was in fact a native Briton or an ex-Roman soldier who stayed on these shores after the Romans retreated. As the Saxons arrived (not an invasion as some believe but small groups roaming looking for land and wealth), Arthur led his small kingdom in defence and over time became rather well known for his military prowess. Tales of his victories spread amongst the other kingdoms and as the Saxons became woven into the culture they too began to tell tales of Arthur whose name was resurrected when the Christians came to our shores in hopes of converting the "Heathen" locals. The new "Anglo-Saxons" believed their world was ending and thus needed a hero to lead them to victory and Arthur was the one to whom they turned. Of course this is just one theory amongst hundreds and like others, I have no tangible proof but to me it seems like the most plausible. I also believe that he most definitely would have been Pagan due to the religious landscape in this moment in history. Whether he was Saxon Heathen or followed the Roman pantheon I very much doubt he would have had Christian leanings for we would have had a lot more written accounts from monastic scholars regarding the exploits of our hero.

Of course as great as Arthur was he wasn't able to achieve greatness on his own; in fact he had a trusted advisor to whom he turned to when he found himself in a quandary. This advisor just happens to be our next hero, a wise old man with the cunning of a fox and the ability to summon magic to help his friends, a name to strike fear into mortal men—the magician, Merlin.

CHAPTER ELEVEN

MERLIN

Who hasn't wanted special magical powers at some point in their lives? The ability to foresee the future, or the power to manipulate our enemies, I know I certainly have! Oh, how different our lives could have been if we had known the outcome of our choices. Luckily for the hero in our last chapter he had such a weapon at his disposal that seemed to have these abilities; of course I am referring to Merlin, King Arthur's famous cohort.

Poet, Teacher, Magician, and Son of the Devil are just some of the titles given to our wiley wizard. Some say he weaved his craft to help those he deemed worthy whilst others maintain he had his own personal agenda for lending his mystical powers. The truth of the matter remains that he is a mainstay of British folklore with roots ranging from Wales to the Somerset levels. Legend has it that he set up camp in Glastonbury and lived on the Tor. Ironically the end shot in the BBC TV drama *Merlin* showed our hero in the modern age walking past Glastonbury Tor; maybe the producers know something we don't! I doubt there isn't a place in the UK that wouldn't love to lay claim to the historical birthplace of Merlin; can you imagine the tourist melee that would ensue? But what do we really know about this mythical figure?

Obviously Merlin is best known from Arthurian legend and the modern image and depiction of the character first appears in Geoffrey of Monmouth's classical historical masterpiece, Historia Regum Britanniae, written c. 1136, and some say is based on an amalgamation of previous historical and legendary figures from around the British Isles. Most modern scholars would state that Geoffrey combined existing stories of Myrddin Wyllt (Merlinus Caledonensis), who was a North Brythonic prophet and madman with absolutely no connection to King Arthur whatsoever with tales of the Romano-British war leader Ambrosius Aurelianus to form the composite figure he called Merlin Ambrosius (Welsh: Myrddin Emrys).Geoffrey's rather colourful depiction of the character was incredibly popular, especially in Wales who adopted him as a national figure. He also informed us of his rather unusual lineage, describing him as a cambion: born of a mortal woman, sired by an incubus, the non-human from whom he inherits his supernatural powers and abilities. Obviously this would explain why the character became popular and how he had such awesome powers. Who wouldn't want to claim such a character as their own?

Over the years there have been many theories regarding our hero, some rather outlandish but others that seem entirely plausible. Some suggest he was a Saxon or native Briton medicine man (as portrayed in the 2004movie, *King Arthur*) others say he originated in Cornwall and used Tintagel as his base. There is even a cave by Tintagel Castle named after him. During the Middle Ages there seemed to be a bit of a backlash against our hero. It almost looks like the Christians seemed to be putting emphasis on the fact that he had a somewhat dubious character and wasn't such a nice chap after all. Maybe the church didn't want the normal people to be pulled away from the gaze of God, as with a lot of ancient characters from folklore during the Middle Ages there appears to be a great deal of character assassination going on. Did he pose such a threat to the non-indigenous religious movement? Or am I just being a tad overzealous in my meanderings? One of the latest theories by author Nikolai Tolstoy hypothesizes that Merlin is based on an historical personage that is based on a 6th-century Druid living in southern Scotland. His basis for such an argument relies on the fact that early references to Merlin describe him as possessing characteristics which modern scholarship (but not that of the time the sources were written) would recognize as Druidical in their nature—his inference being that those characteristics were not invented by the early chroniclers, but belonged to a real person. If so, his hypothetical Merlin would have lived about a century after the hypothetical historical Arthur. In my opinion this could have some merit; however I feel he has the time line a little too modern. As most Pagan' know, the Druids last stronghold was in Anglesey, North Wales; this would lend credence to the Druidic references and similarities. It would also fit nicely with chronological references to King Arthur. As always this is purely hypothetical on my part. So where does this leave us regarding the origins of Merlin? When we look at the folklore and take a closer look at his abilities we notice striking similarities to other heroes in this book, for example Herne the Hunter. A wiley old man who wonders around in the forests, has the ability to shape-shift and commune with the wild beasts—a bit of a coincidence in my opinion, could we not be looking at two different visions of the same mythical person? It isn't such a leap of faith to come to the conclusion that they are the one and same. No matter what I suggest we will never know for sure and to be honest I personally enjoy the chance to throw ideas out there; it makes us question and investigate for ourselves, and that is what makes it exciting.

In my humble opinion I believe that Merlin was in fact some sort of Druid or Heathen Shaman who was well respected within the local area (which I believe to be Wales) and was a simple worker of the Earth energies. I believe he was in fact real and that he held great influence and sway over those with whom connected. With regards to the Arthur connection I am somewhat sitting on the fence and have no real "gut instinct" either way. I am not a firm believer but could be convinced by a rather strong argument in favour of such a claim. I have another personal theory that may seem a little off the wall. Is it possible that the name Merlin is merely a title passed from master to student? Could there have been more than one Merlin and possibly explain why there are so many conflicting ideas regarding his origins and timelines? Again this is entirely plausible considering the power a Shaman had within the Welsh and Saxon folklore and tribe. Alas we will never know for sure unless hard archaeological evidence is found that is irrefutable even to the sceptics among us.

Regardless of what you individually believe is the truth behind the myth it would appear that the common factors within each story is that he was the architect of his own demise. It also seems like he knew his fate but did nothing to change it, could this be some sort of ancient folklore telling us the morals of the adage of actions and consequences? Could it be no more than a tale of social caution? Or merely that all of us can be defeated no matter what our skill set?

CHAPTER TWELVE
MORGAN LE FAY

Call me presumptuous but common sense would draw me to conclude that if you have purchased this book you class yourself as a "Pagan". As a Pagan you no doubt have met, know or even claim yourself to be descended from a great character from our ancient past. Don't get me wrong, I am not knocking you if you do but I myself seem to have a knack of meeting people who throw the gauntlet down when laying bragging rights to their lineage within the Pagan community. I would wager that most, if not all of you have seen or been the victim of so called "Bicca and Bitchcraft" when attending Pagan gatherings or events. You may ask yourself why I should go off on a tangent but I assure you it has a lot to do with the subject of enquiry within this chapter. The reason I would start this chapter in such an odd way is that from my experiences with most female Pagans I meet claim to be the living descendant of one of the most enigmatic and misunderstood Pagan characters we have within the Earth-based faiths, Morgan Le Fay. Maybe it's due to the possibility that these women feel akin to her or maybe due to the fact that I live in Glastonbury which is said to be the "spiritual" home of Le Fay but as with most of our heroes nothing is so straightforward. Yet again we are besieged with claims of her origin and birthplaces the length and breadth of the British Isles and once again we must put on our best detective hat to unravel the mysteries surrounding our quarry.

As we traverse the historical unknown to find clues regarding the origins of Le Fay it is no surprise that the earliest spelling of the name is found in that hugely effective Christian propaganda expert Geoffrey of Monmouth's *Vita Merlini*, circa 1150. It is spelt somewhat differently, in this case, Morgen, which is thought by most scholars to be derived from Old Welsh or Old Breton Morgen, meaning "sea-born". Just across the water in another Celtic land its form in Old Irish is Muirgein which is the name of a Christian, shape-shifting female saint who was also associated with the sea; coincidence? I think not. Again we must scrutinize her name if we are to gleam an insight into her true origins. Her surname is said to be from the French la fée, "the fairy" which makes sense as the figure of Morgan appears to have been in possession of magical abilities and may be classed as one of supernatural female figures from Celtic mythology; again, this would depend on which side of the religious fence you reside. It is highly plausible that her main name could be connected to the myths of Morgens or Morgan which are Welsh and Breton water spirits. However as time progresses later myths and tales tell us she is more specifically human but still retains her magical powers and fairy-like appearance. I understand that throughout the ages all of our folklore has changed somewhat but why would we make her more human as opposed to her original form? Is it because we as a culture were losing our ancestral link to the Earth-based religions? Or was it the rise of Christianity that turned people away from their indigenous faith? Regardless of your opinion, we can't deny that Le Fey evolved throughout the ages.

I have to agree with most historic investigators that inspiration for her character most likely came from earlier Welsh mythology and literature that evolved and was spread by the Druids' Order. Some also say that Morgan is connected with the Irish goddess Morrígan but in my opinion there is not enough supporting evidence or similarities between the two beyond the spelling of their names. Again, this is just where my research has led me and is not shared by everyone.

Within the Arthurian legend from which I would say Le Fay is most associated, the chronicler Gerald of Wales speaks of a character named Morganis who was a noblewoman and cousin of King Arthur who upon his death carried him to her island home of Avalon (identified by him as Glastonbury) where Arthur was subsequently buried. This would lend some sort of credence to her true identity; however it starts to become murkier in later writings. In about 1216 in *De Instructione Principis,* Gerald claimed that,

"as a result, the credulous Britons and their bards invented the legend that a fantastic sorceress had relocated Arthur's body to the Isle of Avalon, so that she might cure his wounds"

In his opinion it was for the purpose of creating the possibility of King Arthur's triumphant return. In other words, he is now stating that it was just some normal cousin of Arthur who buried him but us silly Pagan/Heathens created our own "mystical" prophecy surrounding the return of our greatest king and to lend weight to our tales rebranded Le Fay as some sort of mystical being capable of bringing Arthur back from the dead. Was this more Christian propaganda to lure the native Britons into subjugation? Or was he speaking the truth, that Le Fay was in fact no one special or magical but rather just a bulk standard noblewoman who just happened to be related to Arthur? I can see why a lot of modern Pagan women have likened themselves to that of Le Fey, for she has been portrayed as a woman of not only beauty but of cunning, resourcefulness and power. I think there aren't many women who wouldn't want to have such attributes and again due to the myth they seem to gravitate to Glastonbury where they claim can feel the energy of Le Fey in the very fabric of the landscape. As a contradiction within the Arthurian tale, Le Fey is cast as the main villain during the early Middle Ages. She is described as using her abilities to secretly sleep with Arthur, thus producing a son named Mordred who was prophesised to kill the great king and take over the kingdom. It is strange that one minute she is a "nobody", then a great kind and omnipotent sorceress then finally a villain of whom we are to despise. I personally believe this to be complete rubbish and that it was nothing more than a smear campaign focused on turning the indigenous belief system into nothing more than tales to tell our children. I also believe it to be politically-led for what monarch in their right mind would favour a legend that foretold Britain's greatest king coming back to life, thus usurping the current king from the throne!

Throughout the mid and late Middle Ages Le Fey seems to pop up as a lover for various heroes dotted around the country and as far afield as Italy and again is sometimes cast as the villain or the heroine depending on who is recanting the tale. Once again they are using her name as a political and religious weapon in a war for our souls. I truly believe that the Christian faith has a lot to answer for regarding the crushing of the indigenous belief systems in Northern Europe. However, as I stated, more and more women are becoming advocates regarding Le Fey and have even put her on a pedestal with regards to equal rights and the empowerment of women in today's misogynistic world. Le Fey seems to be a poster girl for those downtrodden women who are fighting back against oppression and her popularity shows no sign of abating; in fact her following seems to be growing at an astonishing rate. The cynic in me also thinks that this could be another reason why the Church decided to cast aspersions upon Le Fey: that they were in fact terrified that a "woman" could be in a position of power and cast influence against them thus influencing people's views regarding their treatment of women in general. Of course these are just my own opinions but I would state that they are in all probability true considering the lengths that the Christians have gone to expand their faith, not only in Britain but also across the world.

Within Paganism and Heathenism there are hundreds of characters both male and female that could be classed as a hero. I believe that Le Fey deserved to be included not just because of the raw historical deal she has been dealt but because of her enduring legacy regarding the empowerment of women. Regardless if she was real or not, her trials and tribulations have had a profound effect on a vast swath of women within the Pagan community and this can only be a good thing. Le Fey maybe seen as a villain by some but to the many that follow the old ways she was and still is a worthy Pagan hero.

CHAPTER THIRTEEN
ROBIN HOOD

Outlaw, folk hero, villain and thief, just some of the titles levelled at one of Britain's greatest heroes. The man that needs no other introduction and I have to admit is one of my personal favourites, the hooded crusader of justice himself –BATMAN! Only joking, it's Robin Hood.

When one utters the name Robin Hood the image that is conjured in one's mind's eye depends on one's age group. Is it Kevin Costner's *Prince of Thieves* or maybe the glory days of the silver screen when Errol Flynn could be seen swinging from the trees in a pair of bright green tights? Maybe it's even the newest incarnation starring Russel Crowe from 2010. Regarding the latter, you may have noticed the quote at the beginning of the book that I find sums up the spirit of this book faultlessly, which may give you a clue to what vision of the character I believe to hold some historical relevance. As a footnote I am from the age group that loved the 80s TV show *Robin of Sherwood,* something I shall come back to later. Regardless of how you envisage the hooded hero you can't help but smile, probably due to the fact that we have all grown up with the exciting exploits of one of our country's greatest heroes, or maybe the thought of a man and his ragtag band of brothers sticking it to "the Man" fills your heart with a rebellious fire. I would also assume that we all at some point wanted to be the one who fights on the side of righteousness and who leads the charge against tyrants hell-bent on enslaving the working man. But putting aside our Hollywood picture of the man what do we know about this historical character? Some argue he never existed at all whilst others throw a myriad of theories regarding the origins of our man of mystery. As always I could write an entire book on this man alone but I am neither a Hood fanatic nor am I wishing to make him my whole subject matter but rather try and shed some light on any facts we might have and maybe once again throw in a few ideas of my own.

In the fifteenth and early part of the sixteenth century, England was awash with bardic ballads recanting the name of Robin Hood and his adventures. As far as we can tell there isn't much in the way of evidence before this period in history apart from a reference in the year 1377 in a text by William Langland called *Piers Plowman*, a character named Sloth mentions that he knows rhymes of Robin Hood. He goes on to say that Robin is a good man. Could this be the first time our hero is mentioned? As the years progressed it would seem that Robin was in fact a mainstay of the travelling minstrel's repertoire. This would point to the fact that the general populace had already began to form a connection to the outlaw and loved hearing tales of his adventures, which I would surmise to be a tonic for the ills that plagued the working class at this point in English history. But could his legend be from further back in time? Could it actually be from the time of the Norman Conquest itself? Some scholars believe that Robin Hood was in fact a Saxon and was knee-deep in a role as a freedom fighter against Norman rule. I personally believe this to be the most probable theory regarding his origins. However I don't think he would have been as squeaky-clean as Hollywood and fairy tales would have him. I am of the opinion that anyone alive during this turbulent time in England's history would have had to do rather unethical and violent things to survive. Just to keep a roof over your family's head would have taken quite a bit of doing let alone waging guerrilla warfare on an occupying force. With restrictions on hunting and colossal taxation you can see why people fought back. Of course this no mere fairy tale. We have evidence presented to us from that awesome tablet of capitalistic propaganda, *The Doomsday Book*, thatefficiently spells out what wealth was available, who owned it and how it was distributed, thus giving us a glimpse into the kind of law that was being thrust upon the "little" people of this nation. I, for one, would like to think that if I had found myself living at this time I would have taken up the sword in defence of my family or run wild through the forests, bow in hand hunting the "king's" deer, or am I also being drawn into the "fairy-tale" that surrounds the exploits of The Hooded Man? Have we all been brainwashed into the romantic side of outlaw life?

There is no doubting the impact of Robin Hood within the folk collective, mainstream media and literature in Britain. Nottingham has statues of the man as well as tours and the like, but who can blame them; it is good business to capitalise on the hero who fights back against oppression, so why not make a quick buck for the little man? It would seem that the only people who don't like Robin Hood are those within the higher echelons of power, for I state the figure of Robin Hood represents the "serf" rising up and taking back what is theirs. On the surface they call him a "thief" and "enemy of the crown" but as far as I can see he only stole what was the working man's anyway! But for all the modern day hero-worship was he a decent chap or a rough brigand, devoid of guilt? From where does the idea that he was a freedom fighter standing up for the working class come?

The notion that Robin Hood was an Anglo-Saxon freedom fighter fiercely opposing oppressive Norman lords became popular in the nineteenth century. It would appear that two of the greatest contributors to this theory were Sir Walter Scott's *Ivanhoe* (1819) and Augustin Thierry's *Histoire de la Conquête de l'Angleterre par les Normands, A History of the Conquest of England by the Normans* (1825). It is in *Ivanhoe* that we are first introduced to Robin Hood gleefully hanging out with his band of "merry men" and the characteristics of said figure have formulated today's notion of how we see this outlaw. In the novel our hero is depicted as a staunch follower of the noble King Richard the Lion heart and helps him and Wilfred Ivanhoe to fight against the Knights Templar. It is in this work that the modern Robin Hood – "King of Outlaws and prince of good fellows!" – as Richard the Lion heart calls him – makes his classical debut. Some may say this is the origin of Robin but when we explore deeper we see that there may be more than meets the eye. Some academics have suggested that there are a number of verifiable historical clues that allude to the legend's Anglo-Saxon origins. In particular, *The Coucher Book* from Selby Abbey which is a eleventh-century manuscript records a "Prince of Thieves" that goes by the name Swain, son of Sigge who roamed the foreboding woods of Yorkshire raiding at any given opportunity. It goes on to state that an Abbot of York was robbed by a "Cursed Villain" and his band of outlaws. It would appear that this outlaw was so feared that the man charged with bringing him to justice (the Sheriff of Nottingham) travelled constantly with a small army, in fear of attack! This Swain must have struck absolute terror into the hearts of the Norman aristocracy if these tales are true; these Norman occupiers had become complacent in their decadence thus never entertaining the thought of outward rebellion. Many modern historians suggest that the deeds of Yorkshire's eleventh-century outlaws, men such as Swein-son-of-Siccga, and their battles against the Sheriff of Nottingham, merged to form the legend that is now world-renowned as *The Adventures of Robin Hood*. They also point out that when looking at the legend's eleventh-century origins we can see a number of topographical clues contained within the medieval and Tudor sources that can be dated directly to the late eleventh century, in particular the Church of Saint Mary Magdalene at Campsall, which was built in the late eleventh century by Robert de Lacy II Baron on Pontefract. To this day local legend maintains that Robin and his true love Marion married at this church. Historians also propose the site of Robin's death as being the hospital of St. Nicholas at Saxon Kirkby (modern Pontefract). Of course these are subjective at best.

Whilst some say he originates from Yorkshire the place that will forever be linked to Robin is the name Sherwood Forest. As with folklore at this time the majority of ballads had real world links to actual places, one would presume to give credence and the air of authenticity to the tale being recanted. In this instance the *Lincoln Cathedral Manuscript* claims to contain is the first officially recorded Robin Hood song (dating from approximately 1420) and makes a direct reference to the outlaw that states that "Robyn hode in scherewode stod." This is our first taste of the link between Robin and Sherwood Forest. But it doesn't end there; a monk of Witham Priory in approximately1460 suggested that the archer had 'infested shirwode'. His chronicle entry reads:

'Around this time, according to popular opinion, a certain outlaw named Robin Hood, with his accomplices, infested Sherwood and other law-abiding areas of England with continuous robberies'.

To have an objective view regarding this statement we must remember that he never named his source for this accusation and it is likely we will never find out but maybe there is a further clue regarding the source within the sentence structure itself. Some have suggested that fact that he used the term 'according to popular opinion' goes someway to suggest that his source may have been nothing more than simple word of mouth. Of course this isn't concrete evidence either way, but interesting none-the-less.

After all this information it may be hard to decide what resonates with us as individuals. In my opinion Robin Hood was indeed real and that his origins lie in Anglo Saxon history. At the beginning of this chapter I mentioned the TV series *Robin of Sherwood* that was aired in the 1980s. I admit to loving this show when I was a child but it wasn't until my later years I realised the amount of Pagan/Heathen references there were within the plot and script. Not only did we have Herne the Hunter but Robin and his outlaws were Saxon and worshipped the "Old Gods" which I find amazingly ahead of its time considering when it was aired. I also find it interesting that Robin himself was deemed a "wolf's head" in the program. Within the English legal system a "wolf's head" (Caput lupinum or caput gerat lupinum) is an outlaw, the literal definition being "may he wear a wolfish head"/"may his be a wolf's head". Could this be an indication why he was named "Robin Hood" or "The Hooded Man"—the wolf's head being the hood? Or could this be from where the term originated? Of course this is speculation on my part and I have no evidence to prove my theories but once again my instinct tells me there is more to this than meets the eye regarding the origins. It may be painfully obvious that I hold Robin as a true Pagan hero, not just because I believe he was Anglo Saxon, and in my mind, Pagan, but because of what the legend says he stood for. I admire those who stand for the weak and who are prepared to fight on behalf of those who can't. Injustice must be fought with absolute conviction and sometimes that conviction can have repercussions on loved ones and those you hold dear. To me Robin sums up the heroic ideals of the Pagan hero and I hope that one day hard concrete evidence is discovered that sheds light on one of England's most endearing legends, but for now I am happy that his legacy lives on.

If we do even a quick internet search we can find that tales of Robin Hood have existed in every century and in each one his story has been added to, altered and embellished to suit the political landscape at that time. The common denominator has always been the fact that he robs from the rich and gives to the needy which is to be considered the backbone of the Robin Hood legend. As a symbol, Robin seems to resonate with not just the Pagan community but with the general "normal" populace. Hollywood would have us believe the "cheeky chappy" persona and have the outlaw fade into the background. It stands to reason that Robin Hood isn't going away anytime soon and I wager there will be many more books written and movies made based on his exploits. As I look around in the modern age I can't help but feel that these times are indeed turbulent and just maybe we need a hero to stand for justice against the multinational corporations raping our planet and governments forcing the "peasants" into financial slavery. Maybe it's time to rise; maybe now's the time we need the wolf's head to make his triumphant return and fight for the little man once again.

CHAPTER FOURTEEN
SCÁTHACH

I would like to apologise if I seem to be repeating myself whilst I recount the history of our heroes. It is painfully obvious that some of our characters are so inexplicably linked that I have to go over some old ground so that I can attempt to expand on opposing sides of the story or try to explain some of the ethos behind our cast of titanic personalities. Of course the Pagan world is full of crossover narratives and most of our tales weave their own wyrd with regards to the interaction of deities and those of this realm. So with that in mind we shall now have a look at someone who has been mentioned earlier in this book.

It's not the first time we have heard this name on our adventure and I suggest that most of those who are deeply involved with the folklore of Great Britain will have investigated our next hero before. A great warrior woman who is said to have taught some of history's greatest fighters, a woman of beauty and limitless martial skill, a woman on whom legends are built, her name is Scáthach.

According to myths and legend, Scáthach, or Sgathach, existed sometime in the centuries either side of 200 BC, making her one of the oldest heroes in our quest for knowledge. She is most famous for being a mythical warrior queen whose secluded and impenetrable fortress was located on the Isle of Skye, an island off the west coast of Scotland. Scáthach, whose name in Scottish Gaelic means "shadowy" appears in the renowned *Red Branch Cycle*, which is a collection of medieval Irish heroic legends and sagas that forms one of the four great cycles of Irish mythology. Some references and accounts tell us that she was the daughter of the King of Scythia, which encompassed parts of Eastern Europe and Asia but during my research I could not find any concrete evidence that could add weight to this claim. For all intents and purposes she seems to have just "existed" in solitude. Not only was she a great queen but legend tells us that she was a renowned martial arts teacher who was reputed to only train the most talented and heroic warriors, the test of which was to penetrate her fortress known as Dún Scáith (castle of shadows), the gate of which was guarded by her daughter, Uathach. It is said that the modern day ruins of Dun Sgathaich near Tarskavaig stand on the site of her once mighty lair. Maybe this is pure wishful thinking on the part of the Isle of Skye tourist board or maybe there is some real historic accuracy to the claim; either way it's exciting none-the-less.

We might ask ourselves why a Scottish warrior queen is so well-revered within the Irish mythology and as if you haven't already guessed (or remembered from an earlier chapter) she was the teacher of one of Ireland's most famous heroes, Cúchulainn. Cúchulainn came to her for training as a test from his would-be father-in-law. He and his friend successfully gained access to her castle and subsequently began their warrior training. At this fortress Scáthach trained numerous Celtic heroes in the arts of pole vaulting (useful in the assault of forts), underwater fighting, and combat with a barbed spear of her own invention.

It is said that upon successfully completing his training Scáthach presented him with the deadly barbed spear, the Gáe Bulg, a weapon feared by the enemies of the one who wielded it. Whilst living with the warrior queen it is said that many a strange thing and test happened as part of his training. Cúchulainn helped Scáthach overcome a neighbouring female chieftain, Aífe or Aoife (who by some accounts was also Scáthach's sister), and forced her to make peace, in the process fathering a son by Aífe. Cúchulainn also ended up sleeping with Scáthach's daughter Uathach, whose husband Cochar Croibhe he then killed in a duel. On completion of his training, Scáthach also slept with Cúchulainn. Some might say that this had been Scáthach's plan all along and that she was in fact in love from him since he first arrived but alas, we shall never know. Like some of our other heroes it would appear that in some stories we are informed that she also possessed the ability to weave magic and was in fact a formidable magician with the gift of prophecy. Some historians and folklore scholars have also stated that she became known as the Celtic Goddess of the Dead whose job it was to ensure the safe passage of those killed in battle to Tír na nÓg, the Land of Eternal Youth and the most popular of the Other worlds in Celtic mythology.

The similarities between her and other warrior woman from different Northern European peoples are striking but we know less of her than we do of the others. On one hand she seems to have a bit part in the greater scheme of the mythology but on the other hand played an enormous role considering her training of Ireland's greatest warrior, not to mention being elevated to the status of the Goddess of the Dead by the Celtic peoples. Some may akin her to the warrior Queen Boudicca, to which I would agree. It is entirely plausible that the time frames may have been muddled up and that the Celtic people's tale of Boudicca's rebellion spread further than historians realised, but that is pure conjecture on my part. Those of you with a little knowledge of Pagan myth and legend may also see a striking resemblance with The Morrigan, the Goddess of Battle and Fertility whose origins scholars now suggest can be traced back to the copper age. It is said that she was a major deity in Europe at this time in history. Like Scáthach, she was a mighty warrior and is seen by many a Celtic equivalent of the Norse Valkyrie whose job was to guide the honourable battle-fallen to the afterlife. In my opinion these two great heroes played a vital role within the collective spirituality and were looked upon as otherworldly but still retained human characteristics, wants and desires. She was also said to be one of three sisters which once again has a striking similarity to the Norns from the Northern Traditions. Some suggest that Morrigan and Scáthach are one and the same; it is plausible but with no hard evidence either way the jury is still out on that one. Interestingly some even go the extra mile and claim Morrigan is in fact Morgan Le Fey; again during my research I couldn't find any tangible proof to lend to that theory.

As with a lot of folklore there seems to be a vast swathe of crossover regarding the trials and tribulations of our heroes, thus it is easy to confuse and interchange events. This of course can lead to numerous theories and suppositions. I am secretly annoyed with the lack of information regarding this mighty queen because her whole depiction resonates with me on a level I find fascinating. In today's macho, male-oriented world it's nice to see a woman who is honoured as a mighty warrior. I personally would love to know more about her but information has not been forthcoming which, if I am honest, has left me somewhat deflated as this is one hero that caught my attention for all the right reasons.

STUART R BROGAN

CHAPTER FIFTEEN
WAYLAND THE SMITH

Every great hero has many attributes and individual characteristics that separate themselves from the "normal" people and each other. Our next hero may seem an unlikely choice for this book but in my opinion deserves to be included due to his near mythical ability to forge weapons of outstanding beauty and awesome power. His name is not as well-known as others featured in this book but not only does he have a special place within my own faith but many who follow the "Old Ways" will know of his name and contribution to English folklore, not to mention great Anglo Saxon poetry. He goes by the name of Wayland the Smith.

References to Wayland the Smith can be found in Scandinavian, German and Anglo Saxon legend and he is reputed to be a metal worker of outstanding skill. Some legends are in such awe of his abilities they name him as the Lord of Elves. His story is told in the *Völundarkvida*, one of the poems in the 13th-century *Icelandic Elder*, or Poetic, Edda, and, with variations, in the mid-13th-century Icelandic prose *Thidrik's Saga*. He is also mentioned in the Anglo-Saxon poems *Waldere* and *"Deor,"* in *Beowulf* (all from the 6th to the 9th century), and in a note inserted by Alfred the Great into his 9th-century translation of *Boëthius*. With such references from a host of different sources it would appear that he was a well-respected man with exceptional and highly sought-after skills. His back story reads like something out of a Hollywood blockbuster, for to think that he was just a mild-mannered metal worker would be a mistake. He is said to be the son of a giant and grandson of a mermaid; with ancestral lineage like that you just know you are destined for big things! But like all heroes, we must first set the stage for an evil wrong doer or an injustice to befall our protagonist.

The story goes that Wayland was captured by the Swedish King Nídud (Nithad, or Níduth) who then lamed him by cutting the tendons in his feet as to prevent his escape, then placed him on an island and forced him to work in the king's smithy. In a plan of cold-blooded revenge, he killed Nídud's two young sons and made drinking bowls from their skulls, which he sent to their father. He also raped their sister, Bödvild, when she brought a gold ring to be mended, and then he escaped by magical flight through the air. Wow! Not someone to take lightly then. It would appear the ones you don't see coming are the ones who are capable of horrendous acts; to be fair to Wayland I don't blame him for doing what he did, extreme times call for extreme measures, as they say.

Because I live in the UK it seems only right to mention first his association with this green and pleasant land. Located near White Horse Hill, Berkshire is a stone burial chamber known as Wayland's Smithy. Legend states that the chamber is haunted by an invisible smithy who will shoe a horse for a traveller, provided that a coin is left on a stone and that the traveller removes himself while the work is in progress. But we are warned that if the traveller turns or tries to watch or even looks towards the chamber the charm will fail and some say bad fortune will befall the traveller. I myself have visited the chamber and have to say it has a very eerie feel to the place, but to answer the question you are about to ask, no I didn't have need of a horse shoe! But Wayland's smithy is not the only location associated to our hero; there are similar stories recorded in Germany, Denmark, and Belgium. There are even some large stones at Sisebeck, Sweden and a site at Vellerby in Jutland that are traditionally said to be Wayland's burial places. It would appear yet again many places are vying for the recognition of having something to do with one of our Pagan heroes.

Out of all our characters Wayland seems to be the well-travelled. Many cultures (even though they are linked via the faiths of the Northern European tribes) seem to lay claim to his origins. Obviously this could be explained by immigration or colonisation but while most of our heroes are firmly based on these shores Weyland seems to be the international man of mystery. Considering he is not your usual muscle-bound hero architype, I find this fascinating. His story, however, is not without a sense of humour; another local tale says that Wayland had a young apprentice strangely named Flibbertigibbet who after a period of time managed to exasperate his master. Eventually Wayland lifted the boy and threw him as far away as he could, down into the valley. It is said that the place where Flibbertigibbet landed is where he remained, petrified. The stone apparently became a boundary marker and remains to this day in a field called Snivelling Corner by Odstone Farm! When I first read that I nearly spat my coffee over my laptop, a funny story in my opinion.

It is in Britain's greatest piece of Anglo Saxon literature that we get a sense of Weyland's true worth and a complete idea of how well regarded he was within the Pagan world, for it is Beowulf himself who confidently states that he is unafraid due to the fact that Weyland himself made his sword and chainmail vest—now that is some major advertising. We must also remember that pictures were also used during the Anglo Saxon period and we have more evidence of Weyland's legacy courtesy of the Franks Runic Casket, a carving made of whalebone kept in the British Museum. The casket is considered to be one of the most outstanding objects from the Anglo Saxon period and not only boosts the legacy of Weyland but shows us that runes and riddles were a potent means of communication for our Pagan ancestors. He really must have made an impression to be immortalized on such an expensive and time-consuming piece of art.

In a time when our ancestors left very little written evidence regarding their customs, rituals and practices it seems reasonable to assume that those of great skill were revered and gazed upon with admiration. In my opinion Weyland was the personification of a hero purely because of his ability to forge immense weaponry. Of course this may seem a little odd to us in the modern age but I am of the train of thought that thinks that the general populace viewed his gift as being bestowed upon him by the Gods and Goddesses themselves; to this end he would have been deemed a hero and attained immortality within the oral traditions. It is also worth mentioning that the ability to "obtain" metal from the Earth was seen as magical, thus adding to the mystique of the smithy in general; of course Weyland being as famous as he was appears to have been at the top of his game.

When all is said and done it would appear that Weyland was a rather worthy addition to our list and I truly believe that his name is synonymous with our Pagan heritage. He was both warrior and artist and lived by his own code of honour, and for that I salute him and welcome him aboard our crazy adventure. As with most of our heroes,

Weyland seems to have been dealt a raw deal regarding his back story and motivations. He seems to have been a normal man thrust into extraordinary situations, forcing him into actions he probably wouldn't have dreamt of in any way, shape or form. Whilst some of our characters have had special powers or attributes akin to magical abilities it is the ones who are described as mere men and women I find fascinating and our last hero has a résumé that intrigues me to this end. He may be an unlikely choice but something about his story makes me take notice; his name is Widukind.

CHAPTER SIXTEEN
WIDUKIND

Our last hero to enter our rogue's gallery is a bit of a wild card; in fact he isn't even from Britain. However, I thought it only right to include him once I read his story. I was in awe of his legacy and felt it was only right to spread his name for the sole reason that he was Anglo Saxon and was Pagan. To be honest I had never heard of him but once I started to research him I felt a little embarrassed that I hadn't paid him much heed. Some of you may never have heard his name nor think he deserves a place in this book, but I feel that once I tell his tale, you will agree that he is a worthy addition.

Widukind (Modern German: Widuking or Wittekind) was a Germanic leader of the Saxons and the chief opponent of the Frankish King Charlemagne during the Saxon Wars from 777 to 785. As the history books tell us Charlemagne ultimately prevailed, organized Saxony as a Frankish province and ordered conversions of the Pagan Saxons to Roman Catholicism, but due to

Widukind's heroic stance became a symbol of Saxon independence and a figure of Pagan legend. Even though we know very little regarding Widukind's life we know that he played a huge role in the Saxon's fight against Christian dominance. Historians and modern scholars believe his name translates as "child of the wood" (i.e. a wolf) although some suggest this is more than likely a kenning than a proper name. As with most heroes it appears that most of the sources of information regarding him all stem from his enemies and like most of the Outlaws and rebels in this book he was classed as a "traitor" and an "insurgent". To be honest, even though the Franks announced he was the leader of the Saxon rebellion his exact military role is unknown, but we are told he was a robust tactician and was very vocal regarding his feelings towards the Franks.

We first get a mention of Widukind in the Annals from the year 777, when we are informed that he was the only one of the Saxon nobles who refused to appear at Charlemagne's court in Paderborn. Of course this must have annoyed the Frankish king and started the ball rolling regarding the inevitable clash. Instead it is told that he stayed with the

Danish King Sigfred (possibly Sigurd Hring), no doubt forging alliances. The following year, the Westphalians invaded the Frankish Rhineland and subsequently fought a bloody running battle against Charlemagne's forces alongside their local allies while the king was busy in Spain. So starts Widukind's meteoric rise as a rebellious outlaw. Between the years 782 to 784 there were frequent battles between Saxons and Franks. History tells us that the Frankish king then committed a brutal and horrific act. The Massacre of Verden was a massacre of 4,500 captive Saxons in October 782 and has gone down in history as a brutal display of power by a monarch. It would appear that the Frankish king was absolute in his attempts to Christianise the Saxons from their native Germanic Paganism and quash their rebellious spirit by any means necessary. Modern scholars state the massacre occurred in what is now Verden in Lower Saxony, Germany. I have to be objective and point out that some scholars have since attempted to exonerate Charlemagne of the massacre but this hypothesis is generally rejected by mainstream historians. On a side note, if you have read my first book *Heathen Warrior*, you will no doubt know my stance on Fascism within the Heathen/Pagan faiths.

So it is with a heavy heart that this massacre became a focal point for the German nationalist movement in the early part of the 20th century, which came to a head when the Nazi Party commemorated it. In 1935 architect Wilhelm Hubotter designed and built a memorial known as the Sachsenain (Saxon Grove) and erected it on one of the possible sites of the massacre. Whilst I understand their plight, I am wary and find their ulterior motives somewhat distasteful.

Whilst the massacre was happening Widukind had allied himself with the Frisians but despite an increase in men, Charlemagne's winter attacks of 784/785 were successful and he and his allies were pushed back to their homelands. It would appear that time was running out for our Pagan hero and the pressure was mounting; his men must have been wondering if their leader could in fact stop the Franks and save them from being Christianised. Of course we don't really know Widukind's state of mind at this point but what we do know is that inthe Bardengau in 785, Widukind agreed to surrender in return for a guarantee that no bodily harm would be done to him. At this point I would like to know whether he had asked the same for his men but it would appear that he and his allies were then baptized together in Attigny. In a twist of logic Charlemagne actually became his godfather! Of course bringing other families and tribes into the Christian "fold" was a well-used, tried and tested tactic to affirm loyalty and obedience. With this one act Widukind thereby reached a peace agreement and the acknowledgement of the Saxon noble rank by their Frankish overlords.

We may sit here in the comfort of our cosy homes and question why he did such a thing and we may have a grievance as to why he gave in to the Franks but we must ask ourselves what would we have done? Did he do it to save his people from certain annihilation or was it that he was battle-weary? In truth we will never know but I like to think it was a decision to best serve his folk, not to save his own skin. Regardless of his motives it would appear that he became a poster boy for the Christian faith and has been to this day even to the extent as being seen as a church builder and having buildings named after him. I know what you are thinking— why would I include him in the book if he gave in and then to make matters worse turned to "Christ"? Well my friends, I believe that the spirit of

Widukind is Pagan at heart and his actions, in the face of subjugation regarding his people is wholly an Earth-based reaction. As a parting fact it is interesting to note that at a play produced by the Nazis in the 1930s produced a wave of controversy regarding one simple line, in fact it caused outrage from the audience due to some claiming it was "anti" Christian and that it was blasphemy. Even though I hate the Nazis the line made me chuckle and was presented by a Verden Saxon leader just after the massacre. It is somewhat fitting that I should end this chapter with a quote that pretty much sums up the attitude of most Pagans and Heathens I know regarding the Christian faith, for it has persecuted many indigenous peoples across the world, most of which have lost their Earth-based teachings. Maybe Widukind's Pagan spirit has had the last laugh after all. The line was as follows:

"That is what the Christians have done; they feign love, but bring murder!"

CHAPTER SEVENTEEN
THE FINAL CHAPTER

Well there you have it folks, we have reached the end of our epic journey into distant realms and explored the turbulent lives of our Pagan heroes. Through the mists of time we have wondered and heard tales of high adventure; we have heard horrific stories of persecution and gut wrenching acts of violence but we have made it in one piece and maybe a little wiser. I hope you have enjoyed our little foray into the world of myths, legends, outlaws and traitors. Some of you may be thinking that some of our characters need not have been included; some of you may think I should have included others, but that's the beauty of this book. We will all have our own ideas regarding the definition of the term "hero". As we have seen many of these people have been labelled with almost every derogatory name imaginable, yet they still stood their ground even if it meant losing their lives, I admire that and if you think likewise then I salute you! Whether or not you agree that these characters actually existed is a personal decision and only you can make up your mind; I cannot and will not convince you otherwise and to be honest that is not my intention. For me it doesn't matter if they were factual, fictitious, myth or legend. I still believe in the message hidden deep within their own personal struggles and by giving you a little insight into their lives might have swayed your opinion regarding the origins of each hero. Then again, maybe you are of the opinion that it is all just hogwash!

In my humble opinion the true test is whether we can see the ethical and humane motivations behind the actions and if we can recognise their traits in ourselves, our kin and those with whom we associate. There is a reason why the tales of these heroes have been passed down through the centuries, both orally and in the written word, and why bards and minstrels have sung the ballads to keep the legends alive. That reason is justice and empowerment my friends—justice for the working man and woman, the right to be free from enslavement from those who would keep you down, and the empowerment to keep striving forward when the odds are against you.

As with all my books there is always a deeper meaning hidden within the text, It may not be obvious at first but towards the end I would like to think that it all comes good and may even inspire the reader to explore their own path. So what was the message in this book I hear you cry! Its basic message is to inspire YOU to go on your own voyage of exploration. To write, paint, make music and tell your story to the world. At the end of the day this is MY list of heroes that have, in my opinion, woven a rich tapestry of lore within the Earth-based religions, manly in this country but in Europe also. All of us have an idea of what a hero is. Some think it is the muscle-bound warrior whilst others think it is the wise teacher who refrains from violence despite aggression thrust upon him/her. At the end of the day it is all subjective; I may not necessarily agree with your definition but that is your business. In my opinion a true Pagan hero is someone who has stood up against tyranny and taken a stand for the little man and in the process been demonized by the powers that be and called a tirade of names to the detriment of his/her family. The truth is I admire every single hero mentioned in this book for a myriad of reasons. Some have stood out more than others have but all had that fire in their stomachs and the "balls" to stand up for what is right.

Whilst I, and I would suggest most of you would rather avoid confrontation it is evident that violence has played a major part in these people's lives and history has shown us that sometimes we have no other choice but to fight back. There are tales of horrific injustices to those who follow a Pagan path and to the "outside" world we may seem like a docile bunch of twig-waving hippies but a growing number are realising that the inner "outlaw" is a huge part of our heritage and should not only be acknowledged but embraced. When we stop and think about it logically we are already "rebels" and "outlaws" due to the fact we are not classed as "normal" because we don't follow the "normal" religions. We are the strange ones on the fringes of society burning incense and talking to fairies! Why not wear this as a badge of honour and tell the world that we are ready to fight if need be? Despite being on the fringes I am noticing a lot of Paganism and Heathenism seeping into mainstream media, an influx of new "sword and sorcery" TV shows or movies seems to be casting a light on the "Old Ways" like never before. It would appear that being an outlaw is in vogue at the moment, whether this proves counterproductive for the Earth-based faiths is yet to be seen.

Violence is ever-present within the tales of our heroes and sometimes I believe it was justifiable; however there are those who have a disdain for violence and see it as a non-essential part of modern life but to them I say this: no one wants the person willing to fight around until fighting needs to be done! And by the Gods and Goddesses we will give them such a fight! Please don't mistake my musings as some sort of macho, chest-thumping exclamation because that couldn't be further from the truth. For those of you who know me personally I do what I say and say what I do; I can't help it, I am Heathen and live to a code. I admit that sometimes it may be detrimental but at least I can sleep at night knowing I did what I believed was right, as the old saying goes: only the Gods can judge me.

Whilst writing this book I have mulled over what I would have done if placed in some of the situations that our heroes found themselves. To be honest I would like to think that I would have acted in a way that would make my Gods, Goddesses and ancestors proud but as previously stated I don't really know how I would have reacted and to say that you would is a little foolish. I have personally known and seen with my own eyes bad-ass hard men crumble and then seen the smallest inconspicuous man fight tooth and nail to protect the ones they love, and to them I salute wholeheartedly. There is no room for ego nor is it a green light to show how tough you are, to throw your weight around and act like the alpha male. It is having the ability to be scared, maybe even totally terrified and still stand fast in the face of certain doom. I would personally rather die fighting than to live on my knees. Would you? Some may view this book as "self-absorbed" or "fluffy" with regards to my ideas appertaining to the warrior and hero. Some may even think it's akin to those self-righteous inspirational quotes that so many people post on social media profiles and to some may even come across as a bit of a keyboard warrior but I can assure you I am neither "airy fairy" nor someone without the experience or skill to back up my assumptions. I am not here to teach you how to suck eggs nor am I trying to preach or convert but merely voice my opinion. Within the Pagan/Heathen world there are hundreds who claim to be some sort of "expert" (I myself met a self-proclaimed 7th degree dragon mage the other day who swore he was the Keeper of the Dark Castle) or those who would ply you with nonsense to sell their book or get you to spend your hard-earned money on a "course" that will change your life. Don't be fooled by these silver-tongued serpents! Do you think that the heroes named in this book did a course or worried about others' opinions? No, neither do me. The Earth-based faiths (regardless of the branch you follow) are within the very fabric of a culture; we can hear it, feel it and sense it all around us, we don't need so-called "experts" to tell us we are doing it right. You may have read this book and thought it was rubbish or you may have agreed with most of my theories; you may even have thought that I, too, sound like one of those snake oil salesmen giving you the hard sale but at the end of the day I am just one man in the greater scheme of things. I am not a "tree-hugging hippy" nor am I going off to eat tofu and chickpeas (no offence if you do). I am however following what I believe to be the path of a warrior and if that makes me an outlaw in some eyes then so be it, in fact I wear that title with pride.

Whilst I was researching and writing this book a very good friend posed to me a question that I feel is relevant not only to this book but to Paganism/Heathenism as a whole. He sat me down and with genuine concern said, "Stu, do you think there will ever be more Pagan heroes for future authors to write about or songs to be sung?" I was stunned for a minute because I had never given it any thought. I had been so wrapped up in the past and concentrating on the present that I had paid no heed to the future and have to admit felt a little overwhelmed, not because I didn't have the answer but because the reality and gravity of the question posed struck a deep-seeded core within me. I truly felt that without future heroes the "Old Ways" and the ethical spirit of our ancestors would be lost forever. It was painfully obvious that future generations would need modern day examples of fortitude to inspire them, to galvanise them into action when the need arose. After a few minutes I said to him the following words and I am happy to report he agreed wholeheartedly. So as a parting word I would like to say this:

Be that example; be the person to inspire future generations and show them the essence of being the hero; be the one who has tales told about them and stories written. Be the one who makes a mark in history regardless of how small or insignificant. Be the one who stood their ground for what was right regardless of what others or society says. Stand proud with the courage of your convictions. Raise your fist in defiance and scream at the top of your lungs,

"I am a Pagan

I am an Outlaw

And I'm not going without a fight!"

In service of The High Ones,

Stuart R Brogan

Made in the USA
Charleston, SC
28 November 2015